Alexandra Smith is the state political editor of the *Sydney Morning Herald* and has covered four state elections and several federal elections. She is an award-winning journalist, including winning a Walkley Award. She has worked for *The Guardian* in London, and is a regular political commentator on ABC radio and TV. She is also the president of the NSW Press Gallery.

The Secret

Alexandra Smith

MACMILLAN
Pan Macmillan Australia

Pan Macmillan acknowledges the Traditional Custodians of country throughout Australia and their connections to lands, waters and communities. We pay our respect to Elders past and present and extend that respect to all Aboriginal and Torres Strait Islander peoples today. We honour more than sixty thousand years of storytelling, art and culture.

First published 2022 in Macmillan by Pan Macmillan Australia Pty Ltd
1 Market Street, Sydney, New South Wales, Australia, 2000

A catalogue record for this
book is available from the
National Library of Australia

Typeset in 12.5/17pt Fairfield LT STD by Midland Typesetters, Australia
Printed by IVE

The author and the publisher have made every effort to contact copyright holders for material used in this book. Any person or organisation that may have been overlooked should contact the publisher.

Aboriginal and Torres Strait Islander people should be aware that this book may contain images or names of people now deceased.

The paper in this book is FSC® certified.
FSC® promotes environmentally responsible,
socially beneficial and economically viable
management of the world's forests.

To my parents, Pamela and Jeffery.

CONTENTS

'I've chosen to keep things closer to my heart until
I figure it out. I love hard, I love who I love, and
I don't make any qualms about it.'
                                        – Khloé Kardashian

1

THE DOWNFALL

EVEN AS THE CLOCK WAS EDGING CLOSER TO MIDDAY on Friday 1 October 2021, Gladys Berejiklian's closest confidants were convinced, or perhaps hoping in vain, that the agency tasked with fighting corruption in New South Wales would not hit the detonate button. If the anti-corruption commission released a public statement at noon – as it had prewarned her high-powered legal team it would do – Berejiklian's political career would be over. At 12.01 pm her supporters' worst fears were realised when a statement arrived in journalists' inboxes. Soon after, an alert from Berejiklian's media team said the premier would make a 'significant announcement' within the hour. The most popular political leader in Australia, who had built her whole brand around honesty and integrity, was facing a corruption inquiry into her conduct.

The public statement from the Independent Commission Against Corruption (ICAC) confirmed its focus had shifted from Berejiklian as a witness, to the New South Wales premier as the centre of its investigations. Despite leading the state through its toughest times in living memory, Berejiklian's leadership was untenable and her 18-year career as a member of parliament in tatters. Across the road in a committee room in Parliament House, one of her colleagues, Liberal upper house MP Peter Poulos, was so rocked by what was coming that he inadvertently told the virtual public hearing that Berejiklian was about to resign. In such a state of shock, he hadn't realised his microphone was still on when he took a phone call.

Before anyone had time to digest the ICAC statement, a red-eyed and angry Berejiklian fronted the media in state government offices overlooking Sydney's Martin Place. There were no tears, at least not from Berejiklian, but her dark eyes left no doubt she'd had a sleepless night. In what would be her final press conference as premier, Berejiklian told the public that their faithful servant, who had not come up for air in almost two years, had been forced to quit her cherished role. 'Resigning at this time is against every instinct of my being and something which I do not want to do. I love my job and serving the community, but I have been given no option following the statement issued.'

Berejiklian, the squeaky-clean daughter of Armenian migrants, had been living on borrowed time. The anti-corruption commission had summoned the premier as a witness a year earlier to quiz her about a secret five-year romance she had with disgraced former state Liberal MP Daryl Maguire. The revelation of her love affair floored even her closest friends. By the time Berejiklian's resignation came, Maguire was already facing possible criminal charges which could have landed him in jail.

The deeply private Berejiklian had intimate details of her first and only relationship laid bare, including recordings of phone conversations with Maguire which, at best, made her sound like a bored girlfriend, humouring her partner's relentless talk of hopeless side hustles. At worst, she sounded like she was actively trying to turn a blind eye. 'I don't need to know that bit,' she told Maguire in one conversation caught on a phone tap. Berejiklian insisted she was not paying any attention to her boyfriend's outlandish business plans, which were never going to amount to anything. He talked a big game but never landed the deals, she maintained. Still, text messages between the pair also exposed the affection they held for each other, including the pet name they shared: *hawkiss* – an Armenian term of endearment meaning 'my soul' or 'my beloved'.

Remarkably, Berejiklian weathered a storm of tsunami-like proportions after details of her clandestine relationship with an unlikely man emerged in the most public way imaginable. But rather than losing support in the aftermath of her bombshell evidence to the ICAC in October 2020, Berejiklian's popularity seemingly grew as she steered New South Wales through its second and more deadly wave of COVID-19. She was seen by some as the Queen of Hearts, although there were also plenty of detractors who were not convinced by her Shakespearean-esque love story. How did someone so capable manage to fall for a compromised loser yet not notice anything untoward during their five-year affair? But her work-aholic attitude and laserlike focus meant she pushed on as premier like nothing had happened. The Delta variant of COVID-19 delivered another longer, more gruelling lockdown in New South Wales. Some of the lowest socioeconomic areas of Sydney had the harshest restric-tions imposed on them, including night-time curfews and exercise bans. The lockdown was loathed by many as Sydney became a city divided. But still the voters did not abandon Berejiklian. The significant political capital she had built through the Black Summer bushfires and the pandemic was her saving grace.

At one stage, not long after her first ICAC appear-ance, her personal approval rating in an opinion poll was 64 per cent. Women were especially sympathetic and almost two-thirds of voters saw no need for her to resign. It looked as though Berejiklian's brush with the ICAC had boosted her stocks, rather than harmed them. The public felt for their hardworking premier, who had sacrificed so much for them.

But when a cagey statement from the anti-corruption commission unexpectedly revealed the probe into her ex-boyfriend had not concluded, as expected, but was instead being extended, anxiety swept through the Liberal ranks. Perhaps the worst was not behind them. Her long-time loyal lieutenant Matt Kean began preparing contingency plans. Meanwhile, the loose-lipped then deputy premier John Barilaro told colleagues and journalists in mid 2021 that he had been called to give private evidence to the ICAC and that the lines of inquiry seemed to be around Berejiklian.

Barilaro had never forgiven Berejiklian after a bruising battle in 2020 within the Coalition over a contentious piece of planning law designed to protect koalas. The Nationals were convinced the policy would lock up farming land because an increased number of tree species were classed as koala habitat, while the Liberals insisted it was about saving Australia's much-loved marsupial. Barilaro beat his chest and threatened that he would take his Nationals to the crossbench, his ministers included, if he did not get his way with changes to the legislation. 'I will not sit by quietly as my own government drives a nail into the coffin of regional New South Wales,' Barilaro warned. The flaw in his plan was that it would mean, of course, that the Nationals would no longer be in government if they sat on the crossbench.

Berejiklian called his bluff and warned that she would march to Government House and have an all-Liberal cabinet sworn in if he went through with his ultimatum. Barilaro backed down. But his failed brinkmanship left him humiliated, and he seethed that Berejiklian emerged the victor. Barilaro took four weeks mental health leave, and his relationship with Berejiklian never recovered. Some Nationals were furious that Berejiklian survived her first round of the ICAC inquiry with barely a scratch, while Barilaro was left battered and bruised over what they saw as a legitimate policy dispute. From that moment on, many in the Liberals feared Barilaro was out to get Berejiklian.

At one stage, Barilaro let slip to colleagues that he was told by the anti-corruption commission that its investigation was now focused on Berejiklian as well as Maguire. As it turned out, Barilaro knew for weeks, if not longer, that Berejiklian was a dead woman walking.

Kean's political nous saw him rise to become a power-broker for the moderate faction of the Liberals, a role he shared with federal MP for North Sydney Trent Zimmerman, also a close friend of Berejiklian. Kean had watched the mortal wounding of his role model, former prime minister Malcolm Turnbull, at the hands of their own party in 2018. Given the damage inflicted on the Liberal Party during the bruising Turnbull leadership battle, Kean no doubt appreciated that it would not be in his interest to shift his support from Berejiklian, no matter what came her way. Kean was convinced it was politically expedient to have clean hands, particularly when it involved a popular female leader. He stayed true to his word and made it known internally (and externally) that he intended to back Berejiklian until the end. Kean controlled the numbers in the moderates, a task Berejiklian once had, and was the one responsible for warning the premier that rumours about her shaky future were gathering pace.

When Kean told Berejiklian about the scuttlebutt coming from Barilaro, she simply nodded, lips pursed. If she had an inkling of what was to come, she did not let on. Regardless, it was clear that Kean had to start canvassing supporters to see if Berejiklian could withstand a leadership challenge if it came to it.

After Berejiklian's first appearance at the ICAC, Kean told his mate and factional opponent, leader of the right wing and rising star Dominic Perrottet, that he would support him as premier in a post-Berejiklian world, but never while Berejiklian was leader. That guarantee was conditional on Perrottet remaining loyal to Berejiklian. Perrottet and Kean went on bushwalks together during the Delta lockdown in mid 2021 and used the time out-doors as an excuse to surreptitiously probe each other for information about the ICAC rumours. Perrottet no doubt had his eye on the prize and likely was not prepared to do anything to jeopardise his chance of becoming premier, and Kean knew that meant he could convince Perrottet to keep his troops in line.

Some senior right-wing Liberals were actively undermining Berejiklian, and she was likely growing increasingly paranoid about Perrottet's intentions, but Kean was confident that he was in the tent. As the chatter about Berejiklian's future grew louder among colleagues and political reporters, Kean prepared a spreadsheet. For Berejiklian to survive as premier, she needed the support of 23 of her colleagues. Kean was confident he could get to 19 definite backers who would never shift their support from Berejiklian – while others would also follow. Some colleagues, however, were wavering. They felt that Berejiklian had left them in a dangerous holding pattern after her first appearance at the ICAC. One, in particu-lar, believed Berejiklian betrayed the party by hanging on as leader rather than leaving when the revelations of her romance with Maguire first emerged. Regardless of the differing opinions, a sense of foreboding hung over the government.

Some of Berejiklian's other colleagues also had con-spiracy theories. The calendar for the final parliamentary sitting weeks of 2021 was unusually jam-packed, which they saw as a strange move for a government without a majority of seats that could do with spending less time in parliament rather than more. It was so busy, with a gruelling fortnight of time-consuming budget estimates as well, that one minister described it as 'hell on a stick'. Some nervous Liberals were convinced that Berejiklian had made a calculated assumption that the ICAC could not schedule hearings into her conduct while parliament was in session, and so she had deliberately stretched out the parliament sitting period. This would buy her more time – Berejiklian could make it through to Christmas and the new year before resigning the leadership on her own terms.

There was significance in Berejiklian remaining leader into early 2022. If she lasted until 23 January 2022, she would reach the milestone of five years as premier. Berejiklian already had the title of the second-longest-serving Liberal premier in New South Wales, only eclipsed by Robert Askin who was in power for a decade between 1965 and 1975. Five years would have delivered Berejiklian a range of perks that comes with being a long-serving premier. The car, the driver, an office and staff. Former Liberal premier Nick Greiner and Labor premier Bob Carr have at times spent as much as $400,000 a year on the public purse through their entitlements. But ex-premiers do not automatically receive the same generous post-politics perks anymore.

Berejiklian's political mentor and former premier Barry O'Farrell introduced rules that the leader must be in the job for five years before receiving any taxpayer-funded fringe benefits. O'Farrell's changes were very deliberate and ensured his 2011 election opponent Kristina Keneally, the state's first female premier, did not get any sweeteners after her 15 months as Labor leader. 'There is no entitlement for short-term premiers,' O'Farrell declared in 2011. After 16 long years in Opposition, O'Farrell surely thought he would clock up five years as premier. That wasn't to be. He managed three years before falling on his sword over a vintage bottle of wine.

Entitlements, though, would not have been a motivating force for Berejiklian. As a member of parliament, and particularly as premier, she steadfastly refused to accept a free lunch, even insisting on splitting bills with newspaper editors if she was invited out as their guest, lest they think she could be bought. Rather, the thinking was that she would want to lead the state out of the latest COVID-19 crisis, emerging as the first Australian leader who managed to work out how to live alongside the virus. Then she could bow out as the state's longest-serving Liberal premier in almost 50 years and give her successor, assumed to be Perrottet, 12 months clear air to campaign for a tilt at a fourth term for the Coalition in March 2023. It would be a noble end to her political career, and one that nobody would question.

There were other conspiracy theories. As well as occasional slips in her trademark attention to detail, in early September, just weeks before her ultimate demise, Berejiklian made an announcement that took everyone by surprise: she would no longer be giving her popular daily 11 am press conferences. This convinced many in her government and the media that something was amiss.

In normal circumstances, scrapping press conferences would be of little interest to anyone except the dozen or so journalists who made up the New South Wales press gallery. But those updates, beamed live into living rooms from NSW Health headquarters, had become essential viewing during the long months of lockdown, even for the most politically disengaged. People tuned in for the latest case numbers, the reassuring messages from the no-nonsense Chief Health Officer Kerry Chant, or even just to take a bet on what colour jacket Berejiklian would be wearing (a light colour meant she had good news on case numbers, dark meant bad news, according to social media). The updates were so ubiquitous they were dubbed 'GladO'Clock' by some of her fans.

No one, including her media director and former Seven Network reporter Sean Berry, anticipated the updates to end so abruptly. Berejiklian's team had discussed moving away from the format – perhaps the press conferences did not need to be daily, or at the same venue each day – but no one expected her to stand up and start her daily address with a message about axing them. Rather than the Berejiklian/Chant show, a prerecorded video from a lower-ranked health official would provide the necessary daily information, she said. As the state was facing a peak in Delta cases at the time, it seemed a very curious move.

Only six weeks earlier, Berejiklian had declared a state of emergency in New South Wales when daily Delta case numbers hit 136. On the day she cancelled her daily updates, there were 10 times as many cases. New South Wales was also about to embark on a potentially risky strategy of relaxing restrictions when 70 per cent of adults were double vaccinated. It would be the first state to take those steps, with the rest of the country watching on anxiously. In 2020, the first year of the pandemic, Berejiklian only stopped daily press conferences when New South Wales was recording very low numbers of new infections. No one could understand Berejiklian's rationale for stopping again now.

Asked why she was pulling the plug on daily briefings just as the peak of cases was expected, Berejiklian said we wouldn't know when the peak was reached. *The Guardian Australia*'s political commentator Anne Davies described Berejiklian's decision as 'a serious abrogation of her responsibilities as the state's communicator-in-chief', while others saw her clumsy line that she would face the cameras 'when I feel I need to be accountable' as oozing with hubris.

The state parliament had not sat for more than three months after being abruptly shut down because of the impending threat from the Delta wave, and it was still not due to resume until the following month. Berejiklian's press conferences were the only avenue for the government to be held to account. 'I will turn up when I need to, but to expect the leader of the government indefinitely to do this every day means that I am not doing my job properly,' was her excuse. Only days earlier, Berejiklian had released modelling that estimated COVID-19 cases were about to peak and hospitalisations would surge in the next month. September and October were going to be tough months for the state. 'It is important for us to get the right balance, to lead and govern and do what is required. Of course, accountability is something we live with 24/7 but how we communicate and present the information is better managed when we present ourselves in a particular way,' she said.

Not surprisingly, the cancellation of the briefings sent her colleagues into a tailspin. Even those in her so-called crisis cabinet, the small group of ministers responsible for the government's COVID response, did not know it was coming. Her fearful MPs speculated that she needed a cover story so she could attend private ICAC hearings without her absence raising any suspicions. That theory was almost too fanciful.

The ICAC had brought down two Liberal premiers – Greiner and O'Farrell. The calculation within the Liberal

Party was that the publicly funded watchdog would surely not risk a third. Many of the party faithful, who already had plenty of cynicism around the ICAC and its power, convinced themselves that the stakes were too high for the commission to topple Berejiklian. They were wrong. It later emerged that Berejiklian did, in fact, have an appointment with the anti-corruption commission the week after she announced the end of her 11 am updates. She gave private evidence the following Saturday, just a couple of days after forcefully denying that the commission had its sights on her. Then, in a move likely designed to calm the troops, 11 am updates returned most days the next week.

Berejiklian texted Kean about 5.30 pm on the Thursday night before her resignation, insisting he call urgently. When Kean reached her, she told him that she had received notice that she had been summoned again as a witness to the ICAC. This did not panic Kean. In fact, he felt a sense of relief that Barilaro's claims that she would be hauled before the commission as the main act seemed to be overblown.

Kean knew a second appearance before the commission would be brutal, but he was convinced Berejiklian could survive again. Berry, her media director, was not so sure. Berejiklian asked Kean to organise a conference call for later that evening to talk through options with her most trusted political backers. Ministerial colleague and close friend Victor Dominello – who was always seen as a possible love interest of Berejiklian – dialled in, along with Health Minister Brad Hazzard and Kean.

On that call, the foursome wargamed her options. Kean was of the view that while it would be gruelling, Berejiklian could ride out further ICAC evidence. The others, buoyed by their leader's enduring popularity, agreed. They hung up, feeling confident. Later that night, Berejiklian contacted Kean again to tell him she had received 'some extra info' – but she assured him that her legal team, led by Sydney's top silk Bret Walker SC, as well as her new beau, her former ICAC barrister Arthur Moses SC, were convinced that she was on sound legal ground. She did not need to resign. Kean told her she had the best legal minds in the country on her side and stressed: 'If you fight, you can survive.' He said she had the public backing her, as well as most of her colleagues, and she just needed to 'batten down the hatches'. He finished the text with a kiss emoji. (Berejiklian was a prolific user of emojis.)

Berejiklian wanted Kean in her office at 9 am the next morning. He texted her early, promising her he would stand by her decision, whatever it was. 'Here with you every step of the way,' he told her. Berejiklian reassured Kean she would be okay but told him to be wary of Barilaro. When Kean arrived at her Martin Place office a short time later, Hazzard was already there, ashen faced. Nothing needed to be said. The ICAC was coming for Berejiklian and there was nothing they could do to save her.

The ICAC's statement on that fateful Friday revealed it had Berejiklian in its sights for a potential breach of public trust due to having a 'conflict between her public duties and her private interest', because she had been in a relationship with Maguire while he was an MP and she was a senior minister. The ICAC was zeroing in on two government grants for Maguire's home town of Wagga Wagga. One was for a gun club, the other for a conservatorium of music. It was also investigating whether Berejiklian allowed or encouraged possible corrupt conduct and whether she broke the law in failing to report any suspicions that Maguire may have been corrupt. It was a devastating statement given Berejiklian had built her whole career around upholding the highest levels of propriety. She was incensed.

She strode into the media room in the government office towers for her last live press conference with a missive to fire. Her close friend Dominello stood behind the wall of television cameras, seemingly dumbfounded. Hazzard, who had been by Berejiklian's side through the darkest days of the pandemic, watched on stony faced. Kean audibly sobbed. Berry stood in Berejiklian's line of sight, as he had done for more than 100 press conferences throughout the pandemic, nodding in support as she delivered her statement.

Berejiklian's final message as premier could not have been more scathing towards the agency that had been established the last time the Liberals were in power. She was quitting because of 'the love and respect that I have for the people of New South Wales and the high regard which I have for the office of premier'. She said the matters the ICAC was investigating were historical and had been the 'subject of numerous attacks on me by political opponents during the last 12 months'. Berejiklian made it clear that she believed her demise was completely beyond her control. To her mind, she was the victim of a political hit job but not one instigated by the usual opportunistic opponents. It was the ICAC that had deliberately set out to end her.

Of course, the rules she had set, and enforced, also left her little choice. 'I have made it clear on numerous occasions that if any of my ministers were the subject of allegations being investigated by an integrity agency or law enforcement, then he or she should stand aside during the course of the investigation until their name was cleared,' Berejiklian acknowledged. 'The reason for my stance was not to have made any presumptions as to their conduct, but rather to maintain the integrity of the public office whilst an investigation was completed. That same standard must apply to me.'

She was also left with no option because she had every belief that the anti-corruption commission would drag out the process and, with a state election due in 2023, Berejiklian knew a premier could not go to the polls with a corruption cloud over their head.

The ICAC has a history of lengthy turnaround times for its reports. The long-running investigation into the New South Wales Labor Party and illegal donations, which provided some spectacular evidence including revelations that wads of cash from Chinese billionaire Huang Xiangmo were handed to the Labor Party's head office in an Aldi shopping bag, dragged on for more than two years. Similarly, the former New South Wales Liberal sports minister John Sidoti removed himself from cabinet and languished on the crossbench for more than 18 months before the commission even announced an inquiry into corruption allegations against him.

Berejiklian knew she could not risk a drawn-out ICAC process. 'I cannot predict how long it will take the ICAC to complete this investigation, let alone deliver a report, in circumstances where I was first called to give evidence at a public hearing nearly 12 months ago,' she said in her resignation speech. 'ICAC has chosen to take this action during the most challenging weeks of the most challeng-ing times in the history of New South Wales. That is the ICAC's prerogative.' Berejiklian was not alone. One long-time senior Liberal said: 'ICAC knew exactly what they were doing. Not a care for the lockdown or that we are in a pandemic. ICAC always plays the politics.' Another

Liberal insider accused the ICAC of wanting a 'high-profile scalp': 'We are talking about some pretty big egos here,' the insider said.

However, there was never any reasonable basis for such statements, or for doubting that the ICAC was proceeding in a proper or reasonable way. In May 2022, outgoing ICAC commissioner Stephen Rushton SC hit back at the ICAC's critics, labelling them 'buffoons' for not understanding the role of the anti-corruption commission. He did not identify culprits, but there was little doubt he was pointing the finger at Scott Morrison, who had repeatedly called the agency a 'kangaroo court', and other Liberal figures.

The Inspector of the ICAC, Bruce McClintock SC, received complaints about the timing of the investigation. McClintock, who has a long, distinguished career as a barrister, asked ICAC's Chief Commissioner Peter Hall QC to provide him with information on how and why the decision was made to proceed with the inquiry. McClintock was left in no doubt. Based on the evidence provided to him, the ICAC had a 'proper basis' for calling a public inquiry into Berejiklian, regardless of whether the timing was to her liking, or anyone else's.

Berejiklian made it clear that she was going out on a high: 'I have never felt stronger, nor more confident in my leadership. I have absolutely no regrets during my time in public life. At times we all stumble, pick ourselves up, dust ourselves off and start again stronger and wiser than before. I have done this many times, as we all have,' Berejiklian said. 'My only regret will be not to be able to finish the job to ensure the people of New South Wales transition to living freely with COVID.' That achievement was handed to her successor to trumpet, only 10 days later.

As predicted, Perrottet was elected in a Liberal Party room ballot as premier. His friend Rob Stokes put his hand up, too, but a public endorsement from John Howard sealed the deal for Perrottet's success, winning 39 votes to five. Perrottet's first promise, after vowing to push on with New South Wales' reopening, was to be a 'Family Premier' (at the time, his wife was pregnant with the couple's seventh child). Meanwhile, Berejiklian confirmed she would leave parliament once a by-election could be organised for her safe seat of Willoughby on Sydney's north shore.

In extraordinary timing, Berejiklian's resignation came on the very day that she featured on the cover of the *Australian Financial Review*'s annual 'Power' edition. Berejiklian, Queensland Premier Annastacia Palaszczuk, Victorian Premier Daniel Andrews and Western Australian Premier Mark McGowan were jointly ranked as the most powerful people in the country. The premiers knocked Prime Minister Scott Morrison from the number one position to claim the mantle. It was the first time since the publication's inaugural power list in 2000 that a prime minister was not perceived as the nation's most powerful person. One of the *Australian Financial Review*'s panellists was John Scales, founder of JWS Research, who said: 'I see Gladys as being the standout premier, the one who hasn't taken the fortress NSW approach.' Professor of Social Interventions and Policy at Western Sydney University and one-time Liberal minister Pru Goward added: 'And not just because she's taken a different tack, but because of the quality of the contact tracing that she's instituted, and then the concerted push for vaccinations as the long-term solution. She has galvanised the debate about having to live with Delta.'

Despite their prickly relationship behind closed doors, especially during the Black Summer bushfires and the pandemic, Morrison was quick to label Berejiklian a 'dear friend' who had displayed 'heroic qualities' as premier in the wake of her resignation. Notably, he added that he had always known her to be a person of the 'highest integrity'. Her Victorian counterpart Andrews expressed the same sentiment: 'I've always worked very closely with her, and I find her to be a person of integrity, and a person that works hard for her state and has been a very important partner with us.' Even Palaszczuk, who did not have the same warm relationship with Berejiklian as Andrews, offered supportive words. 'Contrary to some public commentary, I have always respected Gladys and found her to be good company,' Palaszczuk said. 'When Gladys Berejiklian became New South Wales' first elected female premier, it was a significant achievement for women everywhere.'

When the end came for Berejiklian it was swift, brutal and shocking for the woman who had been credited with saving Australia during the once-in-a-generation pandemic. Berejiklian's closely guarded secret eventually caught up with her, destroying the political career of a woman who had devoted her life to public service. Not that she ever accepted any wrongdoing. Only a little less than one year earlier, as she was fighting to save her career, Berejiklian was pressed on what it would take for her to quit. She was unequivocal: 'When I have done something wrong.'

2

GROWING UP A BEREJIKLIAN

As LITTLE GIRLS GROWING UP IN SUBURBAN SYDNEY IN the 1970s and 80s, the Berejiklian sisters saw driving across the city's Harbour Bridge as a special treat. It wasn't the city's skyscrapers towering overhead, the iconic ferries on the water or even the famous smiling face of Luna Park that captivated Berejiklian and her two younger sisters. Rather, it was the second-highest sail of the Sydney Opera House that transfixed them. That glistening white sail, under which the Joan Sutherland Theatre sits, was the one their father Krikor, a welder, had worked on when he arrived in Australia from Syria in the late 1960s. It was a source of immense pride for the family that Krikor had worked on such an auspicious project. Decades later, Berejiklian, a passionate supporter of the arts, would often talk about the special place the Opera House held in her heart. For her migrant family to contribute to one of the world's most recognisable buildings in their adopted homeland meant everything to Berejiklian.

The family photos from Berejiklian's childhood show a chubby, bashful little girl, sporting a wild mop of curly dark hair and big brown eyes. She was always surrounded by her adoring younger sisters Rita and Mary, Krikor and her mother Arsha. One photo, clearly a favourite, shows Berejiklian as a surly toddler being cuddled by her beloved father. She shared it on social media as a tribute to Krikor on his 89th birthday. Another, in black and white, is of her mother in a nurse's cap posted to Facebook one Mother's Day. 'She continues to put others before herself. A constant source of inspiration,' Berejiklian gushed.

The Berejiklian family photos, released to the media sparingly over the years, could be in the albums of any typical suburban Aussie family in the 1970s. Except, from the time she was old enough to understand her extended family's traumatic past, Berejiklian knew her family was not typical in their mostly Anglo-Saxon neighbourhood. This never bothered Berejiklian because being different was not a source of embarrassment to her. Quite the opposite. She realised she was an outsider early in life and embraced it. It would become one of her strongest selling points.

Her parents were Armenian immigrants, part of the diaspora that began fleeing in the aftermath of the 1915 mass murders. At least a million Christian Armenians were killed by the Ottoman Empire in April of that year when officials embarked on what many historians have described as a genocide. Hundreds of thousands of Armenians died in massacres while others were marched to the Syrian desert where they were left to starve to death. Armenians say it was a systematic effort to eradicate their people. But the notion of a genocide is a highly contentious issue for Turkey, where it is widely seen as a misrepresentation of history. Armenians, the Turkish believe, were relocated for their safety. The Turkish government acknowledges atrocities were committed but insist they happened in wartime, where death was commonplace.

Both sets of Berejiklian's grandparents were orphaned in the violence. Krikor's family was originally from a town called Berejik – hence the surname – and fled across the desert to Syria, while Arsha's family went to Jerusalem. In the late 1960s, Krikor and Arsha, a nurse, migrated separately to Australia where they met and married in the Armenian Apostolic Church in Chatswood, on Sydney's north shore. Berejiklian was born in 1970 at Manly Hospital but there was a tragic twist: her twin sister was stillborn.

Even as a small child, Berejiklian's politics were being shaped by her parents, especially her father. Berejiklian tells the story of Krikor being subjected to racist taunts from fellow workers and being forced to join the union, which he resented. 'He didn't feel their work ethic accorded with his own,' she once revealed.

Berejiklian is particularly close to her father, who she describes as 'gutsy and brave' for migrating to Australia on his own. A formative time in her life was visiting his homeland of Syria in her 20s, where she met her paternal aunts, uncle and cousins. In an interview with the *Australian Women's Weekly* in 2017, Berejiklian spoke of having similar features, the dark hair and dark eyes, to other Armenians in the diaspora's heartland of North Ryde, yet not really resembling any of her relatives in her birth country. 'Here in Australia I don't look like anyone. I look like my dad's side of the family. It was quite shocking when I went to Aleppo and there were 50 people who I looked like.'

Krikor and Arsha did shift work when their children were young, leaving the girls with their extended family or under Berejiklian's care when she was old enough. 'Gladys was the adult, even as a kid,' her sister Mary told the *Good Weekend* after Berejiklian became premier. 'She was the leader, coordinating turns on who would go down to the local servo for junk food.' Mary has always been the brash, bolshy one in the Berejiklian clan. The baby of the family, she went into bat for her big sister during the 2019 New South Wales election campaign when Berejiklian was hounded online by trolls. Mary told one to 'grow some pubes', and called another a 'bludger'. Berejiklian, who counts both sisters as her best friends, shrugged it off. 'I am sure every family has a Mary. You can tell her to tone it down, but that's just Mary.' Mary wore a show-stopping sequinned disco gown to Berejiklian's election night event. 'I think you all know Mary,' Berejiklian told the crowd as she thanked her family in her victory speech.

Growing up in her sister's protective shadow, Mary always saw Berejiklian as the problem-solver and the one who made sure she and Rita were 'aligned to the parental rules'. 'She was a placid, harmonising kind of sister and Rita and I were the younger ratbag sisters,' Mary told *The Australian* in 2019. 'I remember we got chickenpox and we wanted her to hang out with us. We jumped on her and rubbed ourselves on her. She didn't get chickenpox. This girl is an enigma. For us, we got to stay home but that would have been a nightmare for her. She loved school.'

Berejiklian's family only spoke Armenian at home, not just because it was their native language but because Krikor and Arsha felt a deep sense of responsibility to preserve their heritage. 'They were determined to make sure my sisters and I were bilingual and proud of our heritage. But they were equally adamant that we became good citizens and gave back to the nation that welcomed them,' Berejiklian said. Even half a century later, being bilingual is still important to the Armenian community. In New South Wales, home to the largest number of Armenians in Australia, more than 70 per cent of people with Armenian ancestry speak a language other than English at home. While those statistics are not broken down by language, that 'other language' would almost certainly be Armenian. At the same time, the Berejiklians are also proudly Australian. Krikor hangs the Australian flag on the veranda of the family home every Australia Day. It is his way of showing 'his gratitude and loyalty to our nation', according to Berejiklian.

The notoriously private Berejiklian not only kept her own personal life a closely guarded secret but it was not until she became premier that she was convinced to speak more openly about her immediate family. Berejiklian always respected her sisters' wishes to be kept out of the limelight – 'We are very protective of each other. They don't like me talking about them too much,' she once said – and would beg journalists not to write anything that would upset her mother. Berejiklian was eventually convinced that people wanted to hear her story. She gave the annual dinner address to the right-leaning think tank the Sydney Institute in May 2018, where she provided a glimpse into her upbringing, which was loving but also fiercely cloistered and conservative.

By her own admission, Berejiklian was reluctant to reveal personal details of her childhood and her extended family's painful past, which included losing 40 relatives in the genocide. In quintessential Berejiklian style, she wanted to talk about her government and gloat about its economic and infrastructure achievements, but was told by the organiser – political commentator and a former chief of staff to John Howard, Gerard Henderson – that it would make for a dull speech, even by that crowd's standard. Reluctantly, Berejiklian allowed herself to be pushed away from 'core business', as she always liked to refer to her role, and be more open. But the shrewd politician also knew it was important for her reelection hopes. At the time, the 2019 state election was less than a year away and Berejiklian was asking voters to return her government for a historic third term. Given the strong financial position New South Wales was in and the huge amount of infrastructure being delivered, it should have been easy, but in a state that has traditionally leant towards Labor, it was going to be a big ask.

Another important consideration was that Liberal Party research showed voters did not dislike Berejiklian, but she was, as Mary described her, an enigma. So, finally, for the good of her party, the ever-faithful Liberal premier let down her guard and allowed the people of New South Wales inside her world – or at least a small, sanitised part of it. 'The electorate wants to know more about me and what makes me tick and I am happy to share that,' she said at the time. (She did not like her attention to detail and discipline being compared to that of a bureaucrat. 'Makes me sound boring,' Berejiklian once moaned.)

Berejiklian told the Liberal-heavy crowd at the Sydney Institute dinner that as the firstborn, she did not speak a word of English until she started kindergarten at North Ryde Public School. She remembers getting ready for her first day and her mother encouraging her not to worry if she didn't understand everything. She should just raise her hand and have a go every time the teacher asked a question. On reflection, Berejiklian realised that advice probably meant she was an annoying kid.

It took her a while to master the spelling of her own name (and when she was elected it took voters a long time to master how to pronounce it). She does not remember learning English, but does recall returning to school after a short stay in hospital to have her tonsils removed. 'The teacher asked me to talk about my experience in hospital and that was my first recollection of speaking my version of fluent English.'

Former political journalist turned media adviser Lisa Mullins, who worked for Berejiklian in her early days as a cabinet minister after the pair had formed a firm friendship, said one of her favourite stories Berejiklian had recounted to her was from her early days at school. 'Once you could write a full sentence, the kids in the class were given an award on the back of their chair,' Mullins said. 'Gladys was the last kid to get one and I still imagine this little girl peering into the classroom window before school every day to check her chair.' The long-awaited award eventually came and Berejiklian was thrilled.

Each weekend, the Berejiklian girls went to Armenian Saturday School run by Hamazkayin, an international Armenian educational and cultural group. Berejiklian was a keen Brownie from the age of seven and later a Girl Guide. Even as a little girl, being deeply immersed in her community was everything to Berejiklian. Apart from a short stint as a checkout chick at Woolworths in her teens (where she amassed loyal customers who discovered she would mistakenly sell artichokes as much-cheaper chokos), Berejiklian had limited life experience beyond her Armenian world.

Berejiklian adored school and excelled at maths. But it was the school librarian – who borrowed books from other schools once Berejiklian had read the entire biography collection at North Ryde Public – who really made an impact. 'Looking back, that love of reading really saved me.' Berejiklian was school captain and dux of primary school. Her parents briefly flirted with sending their eldest daughter to a private school for her secondary years, but settled on a public high school – the undesirable North Ryde High School, which later merged with another school and became Peter Board High School, curiously named after an education bureaucrat nobody had ever heard of. The school was a world away from the elite educational institutions that many of her Liberal colleagues attended. Berejiklian tried every extracurricular activity she could, whether it was acting in a theatre production or playing the glockenspiel. She was overweight as a child, and her parents pushed her to be active. She played basketball, but her friends joked that she shot hoops like she was playing netball. Basketball was not her game. Nonetheless, she was often given a sporting award for trying.

The rundown co-ed North Ryde High had a reputation for being rough. 'My parents worried because none of the kids we knew who went there went on to uni. They were obsessed with me going to uni. I was obsessed with that too. Not to fulfil my parents' ambition, but mine.' Circumstances meant Arsha and Krikor did not finish high school, but there was only ever one path for a Berejiklian daughter.

From a young age, it was made clear that Arsha and Krikor expected their daughters to go to university. Berejiklian was ultra-competitive at school and wanted to get top marks, but from what she heard around her neighbourhood, she was, in her words, doomed. There was the age-old worry about kids taking drugs. Berejiklian had never encountered drugs but deduced they were bad by the way adults spoke of them. 'Based on what the local kids told me, every kid who went to North Ryde High got bashed up and was forced to take drugs. This petrified me.' Ultimately, though, Berejiklian had little to worry about. She worked hard, learned to be self-disciplined and, crucially, was forced out of her comfort zone and the overprotectiveness of her tight-knit family.

Her first taste of political activism came when she was 15. Berejiklian staged a sit-in in the principal's office when her high school was facing closure. 'The Wran Government was threatening to close down our high school and I led the student protest to keep it open,' Berejiklian revealed in an interview with her local newspaper. The school survived. She later said: 'I learnt about strength in numbers, arguing for something collectively. I learnt a lot about how to make a noise.' Peter Board High stayed open until 1999 but dwindling enrolments finally saw it close. Then, in the 2000s, the school was reborn and for several years was used as the set for Summer Bay High in the long-running Australian drama *Home and Away*. The school found fame, but not for its alumni (which, coincidentally, includes the man responsible for helping Berejiklian win the 2019 election: New South Wales Liberal State Director Chris Stone).

Berejiklian's connection to the school continued. In late 2017, tennis great John Alexander was contesting a federal by-election in John Howard's former seat of Bennelong, and Berejiklian signed an exclusivity agreement for the state government to buy back the site of her old school in that electorate, which it had sold off to developers a decade earlier. It was a bittersweet moment for the premier, who used the opportunity to talk about how important public education had been to her success. The government later dumped the idea and the derelict school site still stands undeveloped.

The bookish Berejiklian was a regular academic prize winner at her school's end-of-year awards, including being named the top performing girl at different stages. She started thinking about a career in public life at about 14, although her sisters joked they thought it would be another extracurricular activity that she wanted to try, similar to when she played the bass recorder. She was hugely proud of her school uniform – a standard public school navy blazer and green tartan skirt – and revelled in the camaraderie of being in the softball team, even if she was no better at softball than she was at basketball.

A hunger for leadership stayed with her, and she was elected school captain of Peter Board High. Her male counterpart and classmate, Chris Trethewey, described Berejiklian as a networker even as a teen. 'We were school captains together and we would go to functions and she would see the importance of connections and development and I would be there for the cake and coffee,' Trethewey, who became a doctor, said of his friend in a Liberal Party promotional video. Berejiklian's lifelong friend Sylvia Zaratsian, another first-generation Australian kid who also only spoke Armenian until she walked in the primary school gate with Berejiklian, said:

'What you see is what you get with Gladys. I've got no dirt on her because she has always been very honest and followed the rules.'

One former Peter Board student, Rachael Jacobs, was several years behind Berejiklian at school but knew her by reputation, in part because her older brother had been captured by Berejiklian's impressiveness. '[My] brother came home starry-eyed from his third week at high school. He had just begun Year 7 peer support, and was enamoured with his Year 11 mentor,' Jacobs wrote in an opinion piece the day after Berejiklian became premier in 2017. Her brother was, of course, referring to Berejiklian. 'Even then, you could tell she was going to be someone,' Jacobs' brother told her.

The school was one of the few non-selective co-educational public schools in the area. Jacobs described it as a diverse mix of Lebanese, Syrians, Koreans, South-East Asians, South Central Americans and Armenians. The playground had myriad accents and dialects, and you could learn to swear in 18 languages (not Berejiklian, though, of course). 'Our school's motto was "Success Through Endeavour". Of course, we mocked it for years. But never has it been truer for New South Wales's first female conservative leader,' said Jacobs.

In a little-watched video posted on the Liberal Party's YouTube channel ahead of the 2019 election, Berejiklian's parents – who rarely give interviews – provided some insights into their firstborn. With a shock of black hair and immaculately manicured red nails, Arsha – sitting in front of a bookshelf adorned with female political biographies, including those by influential American women Condoleezza Rice and Hillary Clinton – revealed that she never had to worry about her eldest daughter. 'She never did something that I thought, Gladys why you do this, always she does the thing right, she thinks for us, for her sisters,' her mother said in broken English. Krikor added that he always knew his daughter's commitment to studying would see her become 'something'.

In 1989, Berejiklian enrolled at the University of Sydney, where she took a Bachelor of Arts and then a Graduate Diploma in International Studies. She later did a Master of Commerce at UNSW. Her sisters followed suit. Rita studied a Bachelor of Commerce at the University of New England and Mary did a Bachelor of Arts.

Joe Hockey, the former federal treasurer and Australian ambassador to Washington, shares Berejiklian's Armenian heritage. The pair have been friends for decades. But while Hockey's father anglicised his surname – it was Hokeidonian – after immigrating to Australia from Bethlehem, Berejiklian has said she would not have felt comfortable changing her name. Hockey, who sees Berejiklian as a younger sibling, once explained that to understand Berejiklian, you had to understand the Armenian Australian community, which he says is 'very socially conservative, and extremely family focused. Much of community life centres around the Armenian church and Armenian schools.' Her story is exceptional, he says. 'She was the highest achiever supported by an incredible family, with traditional expectations for their three daughters. Gladys fought all her life against stereotypes. She would never admit that because she would see it as a criticism of her traditional migrant upbringing . . . [yet] I can't emphasise enough how many glass ceilings she has broken.'

As for many people of displaced communities, family loyalty has always been non-negotiable for Berejiklian. She told *Good Weekend* writer Tim Elliott that one New Year's Eve, the prime minister invited her to drinks at Kirribilli House, but Berejiklian turned down the offer so she could eat her mother's homemade hummus and stuffed eggplants with her uncles and aunts. The three Berejiklian daughters still meet each week for Saturday lunch at their parents' place, where they grew up – a three-bedroom red brick house in North Ryde, in Sydney's northwest. During the pandemic lockdowns, Berejiklian spoke regularly about how hard it was for her not to see her ageing parents. Her favourite celebration of the year is Easter, but the pandemic saw her spend that holiday by herself for the first time in her life. Her separation from her parents lasted more than 100 days.

The only thing more important to Berejiklian than her family is her Armenian heritage. As a self-confessed goody-two-shoes, Berejiklian was an unlikely contender to be declared persona non grata by government officials. But after defying an Australian Department of Foreign Affairs and Trade travel warning in 2013, Berejiklian was blacklisted from entering Azerbaijan, the oil-rich country nestled between Russia and Iran. Her crime? The Armenian diaspora's favourite Australian daughter visited Nagorno-Karabakh, a contentious pocket of land that is located, technically, in Azerbaijan but governed under the self-styled Republic of Artsakh. The enclave has been a source of simmering tension for decades. In 1988, when Nagorno-Karabakh was part of Azerbaijan, its legislature voted to join Armenia because the vast majority of its residents were ethnic Armenian. Despite this, Nagorno-Karabakh is not internationally recognised as a country – including by Australia – and Azerbaijan has banned foreigners from visiting the contested territory.

That did not stop the straitlaced Berejiklian from helping the Armenian National Committee of Australia organise a delegation of likeminded politicians to visit Nagorno-Karabakh in 2013. Berejiklian's parents joined her on the trip (not at the taxpayer's expense), which earned her a place on Azerbaijan's list of 'unwelcome people', something she has often described as a badge of honour. Six other state MPs on that trip were also declared personae non gratae, including Christian Democrats' Fred Nile – an opponent of same sex marriage, gay adoption, Islamic face coverings and the availability of halal food in Australian supermarkets – and the New South Wales speaker, Jonathan O'Dea.

Australia, in particular New South Wales, has a long history of fondness towards Armenia, in part because Sydney is home to about 40,000 of the estimated 50,000 Armenians in Australia. But what is less known, and barely discussed in Australian folklore, is a coincidence the two countries share that has been key to shaping their national identities. While the 1915 ill-fated Gallipoli landings are commemorated in Australia on 25 April each year, for Armenians, just one day earlier marks the anniversary of the start of a round of mass murders. In an essay for *The Monthly* in 2007, historian Robert Manne argued that it was an odd situation that the link between the two defining moments of the national psyche for both Australia and Armenia remains largely unacknowledged.

In 1997, the Parliament of New South Wales took the bold step of formally recognising the 1915 Armenian genocide. New South Wales was an outlier: the first state in Australia to take a position on the fraught geopolitical situation. As well as leading the way in acknowledging the genocide, in 1999 a New South Wales memorial was unveiled in the Peace Garden in the grounds of Parliament House. The Labor premier at the time, Bob Carr, said: 'The memorial does provide for all those that visit Parliament House a reminder of what happened in 1915. I'd like to think that this state – this parliament – has taken the lead in this acknowledgement.' The Armenian community is part of the Australian community and Armenians wear their Australian citizenship with pride, Carr said at the time.

Before Berejiklian's 2013 'law-breaking' trip, another vote was also unanimously passed in the New South Wales Legislative Council which, in effect, recognised Nagorno-Karabakh as a separate country, acknowledged it had 'the right to self-determination' and urged Australia to also recognise its independence. The motion quietly passed without dissent, or any publicity for that matter. Even Australia's foreign minister (who ironically, by this stage, was Bob Carr, who had moved on to federal politics for a stint) had no idea about it. The New South Wales upper house has a habit of wading into international affairs, and had also managed to offend Turkey when it voted to acknowledge and condemn the massacre of Armenians and other persecuted minorities during and after World War I. That motion ruffled diplomatic feathers and Turkish officials for a while threatened to ban New South Wales politicians from the 100th anniversary of the Gallipoli landings because of the state's official recognition of the 1915 genocide of Armenians, Greeks and Assyrians.

Australians' limited understanding of the genocide and its place in history explains, in part, why retaining and celebrating her heritage is so important to Berejiklian, and her Armenian community. The Armenian diaspora around the world far outweighs Armenia's own population of almost 3 million, and when deadly fighting broke out in Nagorno-Karabakh in late 2020, Armenians worldwide were outspoken about their concerns. Leading the charge were Los Angeles' most famous Armenians, reality television stars Kourtney, Kim, Khloé and Rob Kardashian, who used their huge social media following to highlight the ongoing conflict.

'Please share the news,' Kim Kardashian posted to her Instagram story. 'Armenians in Artsakh have been attacked. We are praying [for the] brave men & women risking their lives to protect Artsakh & Armenia.' Khloé Kardashian joined in: 'I pray so deeply for everyone's safety and health. Armenia and Artsakh are defending themselves but seek assistance from the international community to condemn these attacks & restore peace to the region.'

The Kardashians have long been vocal advocates for the Armenian cause. Kim and her sister Kourtney attended the Hollywood premiere of Armenian genocide film *The Promise* in April 2017, alongside fellow Armenian, US pop icon Cher. The film's trailer was played on repeat during episodes of *Keeping Up With the Kardashians*. Berejiklian makes no secret of being a fangirl of the Kardashians (she loves their reality TV show) and she was starstruck for days after an encounter with Cher. Cher was the headline act for Sydney's Mardi Gras afterparty in 2018 and she hit it off with Berejiklian. The international music star pulled out her best Armenian and asked Berejiklian 'How are you?' in their mother tongue when they ran into each other in Oxford Street, home of the world-famous parade.

In 2015, just before she delivered her first budget as treasurer, Berejiklian attended the screening of a German-language film at the Goethe-Institut in Sydney about the Armenian genocide. When it became clear that after the movie she would share a platform with a Turkish organisation that refuses to use the word 'genocide' to describe the events of 1915, she decided not to speak. She later explained to the *Australian Financial Review*: 'To give a voice to people who deny something so horrific and allege that it wasn't a state policy to get rid of millions of people, not just Armenians but also Pontian Greeks and Assyrians, is to me personally offensive. Unless that is acknowledged, future generations will continue those acts.'

Known for her fierce work ethic, Berejiklian had been in public life for 15 years before she revealed it was knowing that was she was alive only through pure good fortune that drove her. 'I'm very lucky . . . for me every day in life is a bonus. I had a twin sister and she didn't make it,' she told *The Australian* in a pre-election interview in 2019. It was the first time Berejiklian had publicly revealed the family tragedy, reluctant to talk about it because she felt it was her mother's story to tell, not her own. She only shared it once Arsha gave the go ahead. 'It was just luck that I came out first. Imagine if you had a twin – you came out first, they didn't make it. I feel like I've got to justify my existence by sacrificing. So I don't care if I'm not happy all the time. I feel like I've got to work hard.'

Berejiklian's early interest in civic duty may have been sparked as she fought to save her high school, but she really honed her political skills as an active member of the Armenian Youth Federation and later as a board member of the Armenian National Committee of Australia (ANC), the peak lobby group for the Armenian community. She describes her years in the ANC as 'helping me become the person that I am'. Haig Kayserian, executive director of the ANC, tells the story of Berejiklian being embarrassed when she was awarded the committee's 'second most prestigious' award, the Friend of the Year honour. Other recipients of the award over the years have included Sydney broadcaster Alan Jones (who at the time was the highest-rating talkback radio host in the city), Joe Hockey and Kristina Keneally.

Kayserian told SBS Armenian that Berejiklian was kept in the dark about the prize. 'We made the decision not to tell her we were giving it to her otherwise she wouldn't have turned up at the event,' he said.

In 2019, Berejiklian was chosen to receive the committee's most prestigious honour, the Freedom Award. Kayserian did not make the same mistake again. 'We told her because we felt like we surprised her a little too much last time,' Kayserian said. 'She made sure she left the event, telling us of course, before the awards were given. Her parents came up and accepted the award for her. She was at the event, but did not want to be there when we honoured her. That is humility.' Kayserian said Berejiklian did not want anyone knowing how much work she did for the Armenian community. 'A lot of people used to ask me what Gladys was doing for us and unfortunately, I wasn't allowed to say. Not because she was doing anything wrong, but purely because she was too humble.'

3

FALLING IN LOVE
(WITH THE LIBERAL PARTY)

BEREJIKLIAN AND A HANDFUL OF YOUNG LIBERAL colleagues were away on a strategy planning weekend in the New South Wales Blue Mountains. Berejiklian was vice-president of the youth movement at the time. One night, after working all day on party matters, the group played the age-old drinking game of truth or dare (Berejiklian wasn't drinking). As the game moved around the circle of friends, most chose to take the truth option, happily divulging their crushes and conquests. Berejiklian was the only one to choose dare. Her challenge was to smoke a cigar, which she accepted. She took one drag. The thought of revealing her innermost thoughts, even among friends, was too much for Berejiklian. Smoking was a better option.

Berejiklian had been working her way up the executive ranks of the Young Liberals since she joined the party in 1991. She was discovering her passion for civic duty when Pauline Hanson, the one-time fish and chip shop owner from Ipswich, stormed onto the Australian political landscape. Hanson had been dumped as the Liberal candidate for the Queensland seat of Oxley a fortnight before the 1996 federal election after she penned a now infamous letter to her local paper, *The Queensland Times*, following the death of a young Aboriginal man in custody. 'How can you expect this race to help themselves when government showers them with money, facilities and opportunities,' Hanson wrote.

The Liberal Party tried to clean up the mess and apologised for Hanson's 'calculated and callous attack' but when she did not back away from her comments, the party disendorsed her. Hanson ran anyway and won Oxley as an independent before forming One Nation a few months later. She delivered her inaugural speech to federal parliament in September 1996 just as Berejiklian was starting to make a name for herself in the Liberal Party. Hanson used her speech to warn that Australians risked being 'swamped by Asians' who 'form ghettos and do not assimilate'. She continued with the anti-Indigenous rhetoric that had seen her disowned by the Liberals and questioned whether Indigenous Australians were truly disadvantaged.

Just one week after Hanson's speech in Canberra, newly elected prime minister John Howard addressed a group of Liberals in Hanson's home state. He told his party colleagues in Queensland that he welcomed 'the fact that people can now talk about certain things without living in fear of being branded as a bigot or as a racist'. There was no doubt in anyone's mind that Howard was referring to Hanson. The prime minister then doubled down on what was widely perceived as a tacit backing of Hanson's xenophobic views in an interview with the king of Sydney talkback radio, Alan Jones. Howard said he believed some of the comments Hanson had made were 'an accurate reflection of what people feel', although he disputed Hanson's suggestions that Indigenous Australians were not disadvantaged. But the prime minister's reluctance to condemn Hanson's views outraged many, including a significant number of the left-leaning members of the NSW Young Liberals; none more so than the 26-year-old Berejiklian. She sprang into action.

Berejiklian organised an anti-racism rally at The Rocks in Sydney and pulled a sizeable crowd of young conservative activists. Berejiklian addressed the passionate youngsters, condemning Hanson's new One Nation party and the anti-Asian sentiment that she feared was bubbling away in Australia. She was determined to send a very clear message, not just to those who thought Hanson's comments were acceptable but also to the prime minister and leader of her party. Howard's immigration minister and long-term human rights campaigner Philip Ruddock was at Berejiklian's protest, his appearance a big coup for the up-and-coming politician.

Almost 25 years later, Berejiklian told New South Wales parliament that the rally remained a significant moment for her. 'I was the first person of any political organisation to come out and condemn One Nation for its anti-Chinese rhetoric and its anti-Chinese words. To this day, I thank Minister Ruddock who stood by me and actually turned up, even though it was not an official party position of any major political organisation.'

Her strong stance, however, did nothing to damage her relationship with Howard. She has recounted her story of having the audacity to write to the new prime minister in 1996, suggesting he should meet with her to talk about issues affecting young Australians. To her surprise, Howard agreed, and Berejiklian said the prime minister was genuinely interested in what she had to say. Berejiklian described it as 'an important lesson for me in political humility and the need to listen'.

Despite having ideological differences at times, Howard continued to support Berejiklian throughout her political career, including joining her on the 2019 campaign trail when she needed the gravitas of the former prime minister to help save a marginal seat in western Sydney. When Berejiklian resigned as premier in 2021, Howard said the 'whole state is mourning'. She has described him as her political hero and the 'greatest living prime minister'. Despite them having a long working relationship, she still only ever refers to him as Mr Howard.

Berejiklian organised the anti-racism rally just months after emerging victorious as the president of the NSW Young Liberals, a highly sought-after position that opens doors in corporate Australia and sets many politically ambitious young people on the trajectory to being elected to parliament. Other former Young Liberals presidents include Howard, Ruddock, Australia's first female defence minister Marise Payne, Joe Hockey and Berejiklian's successor as premier, Dominic Perrottet. But for the socially naive Berejiklian – from a strict migrant family, and who lived at home until she was 29 – the path to the presidency did not come naturally or easily.

A privately educated budding entrepreneur from Newcastle was Berejiklian's main rival. Despite being a conventional Liberal, Kenelm Tonkin was considered an outsider in the party because he hailed from a traditional Labor heartland and had a job in the business world rather than working as a Liberal staffer. Berejiklian, on the other hand, was ensconced in Sydney's blue ribbon lower north shore, working in the office of Willoughby MP Peter Collins. Berejiklian had turned up on Collins' doorstep as a starry-eyed 22-year-old university graduate and asked for a job. Collins, then the state's attorney-general, needed someone in his electorate office who was 'street-smart, hardworking and loyal'.

Collins' senior policy officer, Don Harwin (who would much later serve as a minister in Berejiklian's cabinet), was on the interview panel. He was surprised he had not come across Berejiklian before, despite her being a member of the Young Liberals, but Harwin remembers her as a standout candidate in a strong field. Berejiklian scored one of the two part-time jobs in the office. Collins described the young Berejiklian as 'genuine, engaging and driven'. Berejiklian's résumé revealed she had already been president of her high school student representative council, high school captain and a student editor, and had won school achievement awards from both Westpac and the Commonwealth Bank. 'She had achiever stamped all over her,' Collins later said. She was happy to start at the bottom and work her way up. After five years with Collins, Berejiklian eventually left his office to do a stint in Canberra working for federal Liberal senator Helen Coonan.

Talented she may have been, but Berejiklian was not a natural when it came to campaigning. Tonkin, who had also served in the junior role of vice-president alongside Berejiklian, was more organised and focused, and for several months looked like he had enough support in the branches to become the moderates' candidate to contest the Young Liberal presidency. However, what Tonkin didn't have was the backing of an influential group of former presidents, who some in the party unkindly dubbed 'The Dinosaurs'. The group included Joe Hockey, Marise Payne, John Brogden and Don Harwin. Hockey and Payne were the unofficial leaders of the group. Other foot soldiers included Berejiklian's running mate Simon Westaway and her long-term friends Andrew Parker and Sarah Cruikshank; Cruikshank became Berejiklian's most senior staff member when she rose to premier.

Westaway says Berejiklian's campaign team desperately tried to shake up her image. They would meet for coffee every fortnight, usually at Payne's home in Sydney's inner west, to strategise. The headrests of Berejiklian's car were adorned with Armenian doilies – much to the horror of her team, who insisted she ditch them – and Berejiklian also had a penchant for wearing skivvies. Her campaign team told Berejiklian that she had to change, and that began with her choice of car accessories.

Even in her early 20s, Berejiklian was anxious about not having a boyfriend. Colleagues remember that she would sometimes be in tears as her inner circle, led by the much wiser head Payne, pushed her beyond her comfort zone, including with none too subtle suggestions to lose weight. Westaway remembers Berejiklian like this: 'She wasn't cool. She had a very conservative upbringing and she had a very uncool school prefect type of appearance. But she had all the other attributes in spades.'

Berejiklian's team handed her a list of delegates to call each week to seek support. Wannabe MPs are known to call hundreds of branch members, if not more, in the lead up to hotly contested preselections; but to the ongoing annoyance of her campaign team, Berejiklian barely made it through half her list each week. Berejiklian could be a little flighty, shy and far from brimming with confidence. Even then, 'Gladys was a policy wonk,' Parker, a senior executive at Qantas, once said. 'We would be having tequila shots, but she was more interested in public policy and foreign affairs.' A Young Liberal contemporary from that period described her as 'capable, smart, enigmatic and dour'.

As the stand-off over the candidacy between Berejiklian and Tonkin continued, Payne intervened. Her message to Tonkin was clear: she did not want to cause any offence, but the last thing the Young Liberals needed was another man in a suit. Payne was only the second female president of the movement, and that had been 10 years earlier. The first female president was Catherine Cusack, who went on to be a long-term Liberal MP in the New South Wales Legislative Council. Federal MP Jason Falinski, who had been president of the Young Liberals two years before Berejiklian, said a major selling point was also her ethnicity. 'Gladys had an incredible work ethic but in the mid 1990s we also had the problem of needing better representation from ethnic communities that we were losing to Labor,' he said. 'She also had this natural warmth about her from the beginning. You always thought it was about you, not her.'

For Tonkin, who Falinski described as also boasting obvious leadership potential, this was his last chance to run for president because membership of the youth wing cuts off at 30 years old. He vowed to push on with his campaign, meeting with delegates across the state, hoping to secure grassroots support. Berejiklian pushed on too, with her campaign team convinced she would get there if Tonkin would only fall on his sword. Finally, with some further encouragement from Harwin, Tonkin agreed.

He asked Berejiklian to meet him at a North Sydney cafe with a set of compromises. Tonkin would not stand if Berejiklian gave an ironclad guarantee to nominate several people of his choosing to be on the party's ruling body, the state executive. He warned there would be a revolt from his supporters if she did not stick to their agreement. Berejiklian agreed and Tonkin bowed out. Berejiklian won the presidency, and she kept her promise to Tonkin. Her political career was underway.

One of Berejiklian's Young Liberal contemporaries reflected on their time in the movement and said: 'If you told me in 1996 that Gladys would be New South Wales premier, I would have said, "Okay. Believable." Her or maybe 24 others from our cohort. If you had said to me in 1996, "Gladys would shock her parliamentary colleagues in 2020 when they discovered she had a previously undisclosed personal relationship with one of their own," I'd have said, "That's Gladys. Obsessively private.'"

The Young Liberals attracts a range of people searching for their tribe, including many gay men. The long-running joke in the Young Liberals is that every second president elected is a gay man, and the list of past leaders suggests this is not wildly inaccurate. In the mid 1990s, the conservative faction pejoratively dubbed them the Gay Mafia, and Berejiklian was welcomed into that clique – an outsider who found common ground with other outsiders. Some of her closest friends decades later were from that Gay Mafia, including Trent Zimmerman and Harwin, who spoke publicly for the first time in 2014 about how his private struggles as a young gay man from a deeply religious family drove him to succeed in politics.

One of Berejiklian's closest political allies says she is seen as a gay icon within the Liberal Party, and she has been a regular at Sydney's Mardi Gras parade. She is a vocal supporter of the LGBTQI community and gave an impassioned speech in 2016 to New South Wales parliament as part of the historic apology to the so-called 78ers.

On 24 June 1978, more than 500 activists took to Taylor Square in Sydney's Darlinghurst to celebrate New York's famed Stonewall movement and push for decriminalisation of homosexuality. The peaceful movement ended in violence and public shaming from the police, the government and the media. As was standard at the time, the *Sydney Morning Herald* printed the names and addresses of more than 50 people who were charged. Many 78ers lost their jobs, others were kicked out of rental properties and some suicided. Forty years later, the state government and the *Herald* apologised. Berejiklian did too. She described the 78ers as her 'heroes' and said their 'courage and boldness allowed others who came after them to have opportunities they were not afforded, and to have the respect and dignity they did not receive in 1978. For that, we are all eternally grateful.'

After working for a short time in Canberra for Helen Coonan, Berejiklian landed her first corporate job with the Commonwealth Bank in 1998. The story goes that once a week, the personal assistant to Jill Lester, a formidable woman who had worked in the Department of Trade and the Office of National Assessments before corporate banking, would appear in the doorway of Lester's office at the Commonwealth Bank in Martin Place and announce, 'That woman is on the phone again.'

Lester, who was in charge of corporate relations at the bank, would sometimes relent and speak to the persistent Berejiklian on the other end of the phone. She never ceased to be amazed by Berejiklian's gumption. For four months, the calls kept coming. 'It was always this cheery voice,' Lester later told the *Sydney Magazine*. 'Never upset or haranguing. She'd just keep asking me, "What can I say to convince you I'm the best person?" What could I do?' Lester eventually employed Berejiklian, and could not have been happier with her decision. 'It was one of the best appointments I ever made. She did every-thing she could and more. She just turned out to be . . . Gladys,' Lester said years later. Berejiklian, who was studying for her Master of Commerce at the time, went on to run the tween banking division.

Berejiklian was still working for the bank when Peter Collins, who had lost the Liberal leadership in 1998, called her in 2002 to ask: 'Are you ready?' Collins had decided it was time for him to exit politics – he had been dumped as Liberal leader in a nasty coup only months before the 1999 state election. The state's first female Liberal leader, Kerry Chikarovski (universally known as Chika), took the Coalition to a landslide loss at that poll, but Collins never moved on from his ousting. He wanted to hand over his seat to his former staff member. Berejiklian's response was swift: 'No PC, you should go around again.' Collins was not surprised. 'It was typical Gladys, humble, unassuming, totally loyal,' he wrote in a glowing tribute after her fall from grace. (One of Collins' mates says he was so proud of his protégé, a stunning black and white portrait of Berejiklian now hangs in Collins' home library.)

Berejiklian had a tough decision to make. She had to weigh up whether it was the right time to jump ship from her well-paid corporate job and into the political fray. And there was another complication. Some high-profile Liberals were not convinced Berejiklian could win the seat and were more keen on trying to convince the popular Willoughby mayor and Elvis impersonator, Pat Reilly, to stand as a Liberal. Reilly had been a member of both the Labor and the Liberal parties in the past but was eager to run as an independent. But in the end, Berejiklian decided she would run.

A prominent north shore Liberal said Berejiklian was known, unkindly, as Gladys Alphabet because her surname was so difficult to pronounce and spell. Party officials were worried that her name could pose a problem for her election hopes and as a result the preselection for Willoughby was a drawn-out process, raising eyebrows among some party members. The delay was assumed to be because the Liberal Party's head office was conducting polling in the seat to determine who could beat Reilly, who was well known in the area. Reilly had the backing of former Labor prime minister Bob Hawke, who was a Willoughby resident, as well as former Liberal mayor Greg Bartels. Bartels was the father of Kerry Chikarovski, who had been dumped in favour of Berejiklian's friend, John Brogden. Bartels and Chikarovski were from the conservative faction of the party and never forgave the moderates for moving on her. As well as having the right wing against her, Berejiklian also did not have Reilly's public profile.

On 22 September 2002 – her 32nd birthday – Berejiklian beat three men to be preselected as the Liberal's candidate for Willoughby. It was a resounding win, in the end. She scored 69 votes and her closest rival, local barrister Gary O'Gorman, ended up securing 37. One of the other men she knocked out of the race in an early round of voting was Jonathan O'Dea, who she would many years later appoint as speaker of the New South Wales parliament. O'Dea, a former independent councillor, only joined the Liberals to help his school mate Joe Hockey win the federal seat of North Sydney. O'Dea insists that Berejiklian won the preselection with Hockey's support, although Berejiklian's close friends are still convinced that Hockey backed O'Dea. Regardless, once Berejiklian was the candidate for Willoughby, Hockey threw everything at helping her win the seat. Berejiklian's sisters also roped in everyone they knew to help, including much of Sydney's Armenian community.

Very soon after she was preselected, Hockey discovered that polling for Berejiklian was a 'disaster'. Her team wasted no time in binning thousands of dollars worth of posters that focused on her surname. Still concerned it would be too tricky for voters, they decided to shrink the letters of 'Berejiklian' and go big with 'Gladys'. Their decision had another benefit: Berejiklian was convinced it would make her more approachable. She became known as Gladys for most of her time in public life. Her team also sourced a minivan and plastered it with 'Gladys for Willoughby' signage. It doubled as a mobile office for Berejiklian so she could travel around the electorate and meet as many voters as possible.

John Ryan, who was Liberal deputy leader in the New South Wales Legislative Council at the time, helped with her campaign. Ryan had known Berejiklian from their Young Liberal days but learnt two key things from that campaign: parking is almost impossible in Willoughby, and Berejiklian could be a slob. 'I know you wouldn't think it, but Gladys' car was an absolute mess. But the thing that struck me was the epic number of parking fines she had. I am not talking one or two, I mean 20 to 30 all piled up in her car,' Ryan said. 'She would throw them in the back and say she would worry about them later. I had a sense those fines were thrown in the back of her car, along with piles and piles of other papers, and never seen again.'

Ryan said the Liberals were on the nose in Willoughby at the time, especially because the retiring member Collins had been dumped as leader just months before the last election, and the party had been languishing in Opposition. 'It was quite confronting when we were out doorknocking to walk up the driveways of some very wealthy people in Willoughby and older blue rinse ladies in pearls would tell us they weren't voting Liberal this time. But Gladys was always incredibly pleasant and didn't let it bother her.' Ryan said the campaign was far from sophisticated, with a stock-standard mailout to voters about the most adventurous tactic they tried.

Meanwhile, journalist-turned-consultant Megan Brodie worked on Reilly's campaign, a big spending effort rumoured to cost more than $160,000. Reilly's long involvement in the community meant he had significant fundraising pull. Brodie remembers arriving early at Willoughby Public School on election day in 2003. The Liberals had beaten her to it and covered every available space around the perimeter of the school with a Gladys poster. Berejiklian's Armenian Army, as they were known during the campaign, turned up en masse. Brodie says a group of young Armenian 'thugs' surrounded her. 'Are you scared yet?' they asked. Brodie felt a little uneasy and called her campaign manager, who reassured her that they were all talk. She ignored the young guys and continued setting up for polling day. 'They disappeared and next a carload of girls, beautiful girls, turned up in blue Gladys T-shirts. One told me she was Armenian and had been brought in from Parramatta to help. Gladys definitely relied on her Armenian Army from across Sydney.'

Brodie says there were some dirty tricks in the campaign, including when some volunteers were spotted sporting yellow T-shirts. Reilly's colour scheme was blue and yellow and Brodie suspects the Liberals were deliberately trying to confuse voters. But Reilly's campaign was also not free from skulduggery. Hockey accused Reilly and his supporters of playing 'dirty politics'. 'The personal attacks on Gladys Berejiklian by Pat and his cohorts, both inside and outside the media, are some of the grubbiest politics I have ever seen,' Hockey told the *North Shore Times* in the lead up to the election. Reilly hit back. 'I have no knowledge of anybody entering into grubby statements regarding the Liberal candidate,' Reilly said at the time. 'If anything, I believe the shoe has been on the other foot.'

On election night, Reilly was ahead by more than 400 votes and was so convinced he had won the seat that when his campaign team turned up to his 'victory' party in a club in Willoughby, Reilly was dressed as Elvis ready to perform for his supporters. Horrified, Brodie pushed him away from the TV crews who were there for an interview and ordered him to put a suit back on and act more like an MP-in-waiting. While Reilly was clearly in the lead that night, Hockey warned: 'Anyone claiming victory at the moment is an idiot.'

The count dragged on for almost a fortnight as postal votes came in and recounts were done. Berejiklian's father, her biggest supporter, was stressed as he waited for the results. Barry O'Farrell, who did not know Berejiklian well at that stage, was a scrutineer for the Liberals. He would ring her every day at 3 pm to update her on the count.

'I remember one day she said to me, "I'm going to lose, just tell me I am going to lose and don't keep giving me hope."' O'Farrell laughed and told her to relax because there was still a long way to go. He reflected: 'I think that was what made her a good local member and a good minister. She had self-doubt, and didn't think she had all the answers.' John Ryan, who was also helping with the count, says in the end he was convinced it was a large number of overseas postal votes cast from Hong Kong that saved Berejiklian. Not because they were voting for her; their support was with the Labor candidate. But it meant Reilly was not picking up extras.

Eventually Reilly slipped behind in the count and Berejiklian snuck over the line by just 144 votes to claim the seat. She was one of six new MPs on the Opposition benches. Another newcomer was Andrew Constance, who would go on to be treasurer and transport minister. Constance and Berejiklian were described as frenemies throughout their careers, although she was master of ceremonies at his first wedding and the pair would some-times play a round of golf.

Berejiklian later framed the official record from the electoral commission and had it on display on a bookshelf in her ministerial office, next to a *Madam President* Barbie doll and a child's drawing of her in a superhero cape. Her Willoughby results were a daily reminder to 'never take anyone for granted'.

In her inaugural speech to parliament, delivered on her mother's birthday, Berejiklian thanked her parents for making her believe that the 'sky's the limit' and her sisters for being her number one supporters. 'This includes being proud of my surname. I thank the good people of Willoughby who voted for me, even though they could not pronounce it,' she said.

A north shore Liberal who has known Berejiklian for decades said he had never seen someone work so hard, or so diligently, in her early years as an MP. Acutely aware that she had only won Willoughby by the skin of her teeth, Berejiklian stayed back in her electorate office after her day wrapped up and worked the phones. She called as many of her constituents as she could, to simply introduce herself as Gladys and ask for any feedback on issues in the electorate. 'For two terms, she went to the opening of an envelope just so people knew who she was.'

Her long-time friend John Brogden tells the story of Berejiklian turning up to his office as a brand new MP with a business plan for her Willoughby electorate. Brogden, aged 33 at the time, was leader of the Opposition and had just lost the state election. Had he managed to beat Labor, which at that point was still a force under long-serving premier Bob Carr, he would have been the state's youngest ever premier. He called his six new MPs in, one by one, for a chat. Brogden was bemused by Berejiklian's industriousness. 'I said, "I'm going to frame this, Gladys, because this is the first and last business plan for an electorate I'm ever going to get." She'd done homework that she wasn't even asked for.' Within 18 months, Berejiklian was on Brogden's frontbench.

4

THE RISE OF BEREJIKLIAN

BEREJIKLIAN WAS ONE OF THE GUESTS ON THE ABC'S election night panel in 2011, alongside host and seasoned political interviewer Kerry O'Brien. An elated premier-elect Barry O'Farrell was celebrating at Parramatta Leagues Club in Sydney's western suburbs – a deliberate shift from the Liberals' preferred location of the Sofitel Wentworth in the CBD, where John Howard had always hosted his election night events.

The cameras crossed live to a triumphant O'Farrell but to O'Brien's astonishment, O'Farrell refused to be interviewed by him, declaring instead, 'I'm only going to talk to Gladys.' Within seconds, 'I'm only talking to Gladys' was all over social media and by the next day, it was on T-shirts. Berejiklian looked coy. 'You've done a great job through this campaign, you've done a great job as shadow minister, you'll be a great minister for transport,' O'Farrell professed on live television. Berejiklian giggled.

O'Farrell, who went on to be Australia's High Commissioner to India after his political career spectacularly ended, always knew Berejiklian had enormous talent, but that did not stop others in his inner circle doubting her ability. 'I was counselled by two of my senior colleagues that I shouldn't appoint her as transport minister. They said it was too big a portfolio, she wouldn't be across the details and she wouldn't be able to deal with the union because the unions wouldn't deal with a woman. I said, thank you very much, and appointed her.' Berejiklian, as it turned out, was one of O'Farrell's most capable ministers and developed strong relations with the unions – so much so that the head of the Rail, Tram and Bus Union Alex Claassens and Berejiklian were viewed as friends rather than adversaries. Claassens respected Berejiklian and praised her open door policy with the unions. Berejiklian had only held the transport minister's job for a little over a week when Sydney's train network ground to a halt. Thousands and thousands of furious commuters, who had been let down by years of problems under a worn-out Labor government, were forced to walk kilometres to work after the system collapsed in the morning peak hour. Berejiklian knew it was a public relations disaster for a shiny new government that had promised the world to weary commuters.

Even her friends, who were also frustrated and delayed, were texting the newly promoted minister with their complaints, and all the radio news bulletins were running stories about the debacle. By 11.45 am Berejiklian was at Central Station fronting the media with rail bureaucrat Andy Byford, a British public transport zealot who had previously worked for the London Underground. It was a baptism of fire for the new minister, who had arguably the toughest job in O'Farrell's new cabinet (some colleagues unhelpfully called it a 'triple decker shit sandwich').

Berejiklian had sharpened her media performances after eight years of being a relentless and skilled attack dog in Opposition, which had cemented her place as one of O'Farrell's most reliable and favoured team members. But she seemed spooked by her first big moment on the main stage. The media wanted blood after listening to her over so many years criticise Labor's many failings. Berejiklian's debut landed her 'deer in the headlights' reviews by reporters and her less than commanding performance on the TV news was commented on inside the Liberal Party. Even her choice of outfit was critiqued, with her jaunty red jacket and colourful skirt raising eyebrows; it was unkindly described by one Liberal as 'unfortunate'. Her former staff members still regard that press conference as one of the worst she faced as transport minister.

Regardless of the less than glowing feedback, she stood by her decision to front the cameras with Byford, who made a name for himself as a hands-on boss, spending time at train stations and depots and often writing letters to newspaper editors to apologise for Sydney's chronically late trains. When Berejiklian reflected on that day she was glad to be on the front foot when she could have dismissed the mess as a Labor legacy. 'I felt really bad for people who were stuck out there going nowhere. As the minister you can't shirk it. People look to you from day one, and rightly so.' Standing side-by-side with a public servant was an undertaking she stuck to religiously throughout her career, ramping it up during the 2019–2020 Black Summer bushfires with rural fire chief Shane Fitzsimmons, and even more so in the pandemic with Chief Health Officer Kerry Chant, who became almost as recognisable as Berejiklian.

Berejiklian hit the ground running the moment she left Government House after being sworn in as transport minister in April 2011. Her staff say she did not stop for the next four years. On day one of the job, she gave her newly appointed policy guru Larry McGrath a handwritten note with six major transport projects the energetic new minister was determined to deliver during her time in the portfolio. The list was as overwhelming as it was ambitious. It included a cashless ticketing system that Labor had promised to deliver in time for the Sydney Olympics more than a decade earlier, a driverless metro to the northwest of the city and her pet project, light rail.

Author and passionate republican Peter FitzSimons had dinner with Berejiklian and Joe Hockey in the lead up to the Coalition's 2011 election win. FitzSimons first met Berejiklian when she was Young Liberal president and she asked him to speak to the Young Liberals about the republican movement. The pair struck up a friendship and over the next 25 years, FitzSimons and his wife, television presenter Lisa Wilkinson, often invited Berejiklian to their home. FitzSimons recounts that over dessert at the 2011 dinner, Hockey gave his protégé a piece of advice, telling Berejiklian that the test of how well she performed in the transport gig would be measured on the extent of light rail she could deliver for Sydney during her time in the job. Berejiklian was already well aware of her KPIs and was steadfastly committed to returning trams to Sydney's streets.

Sydney's tram network already ran from Central Station to the city's inner west when the Coalition swept to power. The bold plan to build a second line, from Circular Quay, along the city's major artery of George Street, and then on to the eastern suburbs, was Berejiklian's baby, born out of optimism to transform the city's transport network after years of neglect. But there was a major snag in her grand plan. The existing inner west tram line was privately owned, which meant the government's CBD line could not be linked to the inner west tracks or be integrated into the city's long-awaited cashless ticketing system. Top secret talks were held, and Larry McGrath and senior Treasury boffin Peter Regan cooked up a plan over a beer at the London Hotel in Balmain to launch a $20 million hostile takeover of the company that owned the existing light rail and the city's monorail. Berejiklian managed to engineer a nationalisation that ensured the viability of her light rail, a surprising move for a conservative government much more inclined to sell public transport than buy it.

Berejiklian may have had an unwavering belief in the light rail project, but even her dogged determination did not stop unrelenting opposition from her government's own independent advisory board on infrastructure. The former top bureaucrat Paul Broad, who ran Infrastructure NSW, loathed the idea and uncharitably described the tram line as a toy and nothing more than a vanity project. Nick Greiner, who chaired the agency, warned that the project would have 'catastrophic' consequences for the city's traffic. Rather than taking buses off Sydney's shopper-laden George Street and replacing them with trams, Broad and Greiner came up with a competing idea to build a $2 billion underground bus tunnel running off the Harbour Bridge and under Wynyard and Town Hall train stations. Their plan was largely laughed off, not least because there had been a recent spate of bus fires so the idea of putting hundreds of buses in a tunnel underground sounded safety alarm bells for many.

Berejiklian was never deterred by Broad and Greiner's criticism and stood up to the powerful men in her agency, determined to deliver the project that she believed in. This came with inherent political risks (the Liberals ended up losing the beachside electorate of Coogee, in part because the light rail project caused so much division in that community). O'Farrell and Berejiklian announced the CBD light rail in 2012. It became one of the most prominent public transport projects in the country, although at times for the wrong reasons. There were cost blowouts and delays in delivery; small businesses collapsed after years of being strangled by construction; and there was a high-profile legal battle with the Spanish company building the line.

When it eventually opened in December 2019 – a year behind schedule and at almost twice the planned cost – opponents were still bemoaning that it would be a ghost train. Instead, the line transformed the once-choked George Street, although its real benefit to the city was not immediately obvious because the COVID-19 pandemic meant commuters and university students were nowhere to be seen. The delivery of the long-promised light rail defined Berejiklian's time as transport minister and also revealed a steely resolve that she would need in the tougher times to come. Later, as premier, she told McGrath that the light rail was the achievement of which she was most proud. The night before the light rail opened, Berejiklian celebrated with McGrath and his young family, and arranged a VIP ticket for him to ride the first tram along George Street.

Berejiklian and McGrath travelled to Hong Kong and Japan in 2012 on a fact-finding mission to learn about both countries' world-famous metro systems. As well as the light rail, the Coalition had also committed to building a driverless metro line to the public transport wasteland of Sydney's northwest. A visiting dignitary from Australia was no big deal in Hong Kong, and the pair were left to make their own way to their hotel in a taxi from the airport. It was a very different reception when they arrived in Tokyo a few days later. It was the first time in decades that a New South Wales state minister had formally visited the Japanese city and Berejiklian and McGrath were treated like royalty. The embassy sent cars to collect them from the airport and whisked them off to the five-star Four Seasons Hotel on the outskirts of Tokyo. When they arrived, the hotel's front of house staff were outside to greet them. The general manager met Berejiklian and McGrath to tell them he had upgraded their rooms. Berejiklian was given the presidential suite, and McGrath the none-too-shabby junior suite. But the best room in the hotel – complete with a massive dining room and several bathrooms – embarrassed the modest, no-frills Berejiklian. She immediately called McGrath and told him she would feel much more comfortable with a smaller, simpler room and convinced him to swap. Berejiklian took the smaller one, and McGrath spent two nights in the best room of his life.

The next year, the pair travelled to France to inspect the light rail system in Bordeaux. As Berejiklian and McGrath checked in at the Qantas desk in Sydney, they were told that the airline's chief executive Alan Joyce had upgraded the minister to first class. Berejiklian asked if McGrath would be upgraded too, but was given a swift no. Berejiklian refused to fly first class if her staff member was back in business, and insisted on being downgraded. The pair flew business, and a fortunate economy class passenger was moved to the very front of the plane. One of Berejiklian's defining characteristics, according to those who know her well, is that unlike plenty of her political peers she actively avoids perks.

On 16 April 2014, Berejiklian was in an early morning meeting with McGrath, by then her chief of staff, and Rodd Staples, the architect of Sydney's metro rail, when O'Farrell called his transport minister's mobile phone. Berejiklian walked to the other side of the room to take his call. Not long after, Berejiklian turned around and covered her mouth in shock. The enormity of the situation was not lost on anyone in the room when the prudish Berejiklian dropped the f-word. O'Farrell had called to tell her that he was resigning that morning and she should get ready to take on the top job. Berejiklian had his full support.

O'Farrell's resignation came after his unequivocal denial to the ICAC that he had received a $3000 bottle of wine shortly after the 2011 election. It turned out he had suffered a 'massive memory fail' when a thankyou note for the wine, handwritten by O'Farrell, emerged. He had in fact received a bottle of 1959 Penfolds Grange, a thoughtful gift commemorating the year he was born. O'Farrell was convinced that if he did not resign, he would hand the Opposition ammunition to question the government's integrity. He had spent the best part of two decades levelling accusations of impropriety at the Labor Party. He was not going to give them the satisfaction of returning serve.

Immediately after O'Farrell's call to Berejiklian, her factional praetorian guard, led by Matt Kean, sprang into action and huddled in her office. Berejiklian had taken the ruthlessly ambitious 29-year-old Kean under her wing when he was elected to New South Wales parliament in 2011 as the member for Hornsby, on Sydney's upper north shore. The pair came from very different backgrounds but shared the same social progressiveness as well as Liberal tribalism. An old boy of Saint Ignatius' College Riverview – a breeding ground for politicians including Tony Abbott and Barnaby Joyce – Kean took the well-worn path of being active in the Young Liberals before working for Berejiklian's good friend and one-time New South Wales Liberal leader John Brogden. Kean did a stint as an accountant at PwC so he would not be accused of being a party hack, but by the time he entered parliament, he had already cut his political teeth with some powerful figures in the Liberal Party.

Kean and Berejiklian's long-term moderate ally Don Harwin were in charge of coordinating her leadership bid, although at one point Harwin excitedly skipped off because he had been asked to stand in for O'Farrell, who had been due to meet Prince William, Kate and baby George who were landing in Sydney that day. Throughout the day, other supporters dropped in to Berejiklian's office, including left-wing warriors Stuart Ayres (partner of Marise Payne) and Andrew Constance, although he also wandered into Mike Baird's camp. Baird was treasurer at the time and someone O'Farrell may well have seen as a leadership threat. Soon after taking government in 2011, O'Farrell stripped Baird of responsibility for land, gaming and payroll taxes. 'Mike Baird becomes NSW's least powerful Treasurer' read one headline. Baird was relegated to number 11 on the cabinet list, which ranks ministers based on seniority.

In the afternoon after O'Farrell's resignation, Berejiklian worked the phones, and as her team tallied up supporters on a whiteboard, it was clear that Berejiklian had more than enough backing within her parliamentary party to win a ballot for the leadership. One of the first MPs to declare support for Berejiklian was Daryl Maguire. Kean remembers finding it odd that Maguire would be such a firm backer of Berejiklian, but they were happy to welcome anyone into their fold if it benefitted her. A photo of the whiteboard, which her supporters have as a keepsake, shows she had 35 votes, Baird had 25. Berejiklian was on track to becoming the next premier of New South Wales.

Late in the day that O'Farrell resigned as premier, Baird asked Berejiklian to come to his office for a chat. Kean told Berejiklian that she should stand her ground and insist that Baird come to her, given she was the front-runner for the leadership. Too polite, Berejiklian ignored Kean and went to Baird's office to tell him she was confident she had the numbers to beat him, and she would be contesting the ballot. Berejiklian's supporters said she told them that Baird laughed at her, which incensed them. Baird denied her version of events and insisted Berejiklian never told him she intended to contest the position. 'Gladys came to me and said she would not run if I ran. She said people were running around like crazy which we both found amusing. I said I needed to speak with my family but if I did run I would want her as my deputy,' was Baird's recollection of that day. Berejiklian's staff members left work late that night expecting to return the next day with their boss as the premier-elect.

Kean and Harwin stayed back even later than the others and discussed what was likely to happen. Both feared Berejiklian would cave.

They were right. Overnight Berejiklian had a change of heart. Those closest to her suspected she would have been tearing herself apart over the idea of denying Baird the leadership. To many, he was the most ambitious man in O'Farrell's cabinet and even some close friends say he saw himself as born to rule. Berejiklian knew that outside the parliament party room, the banker from the beaches, with boyish good looks and a Liberal Party pedigree (his father Bruce was the minister for Sydney's Olympic bid and later a federal MP), had broader appeal. She may have had the majority of MPs on her side but Magic Mike, as he would come to be known, had the star quality.

There was also another sticking point. Even though he was a moderate, Baird managed to straddle both left and right factions, which made him palatable to the conservative arm of the party, who had long viewed the progressive Berejiklian with suspicion. She confided in colleagues that she feared that the right wing of the party would never accept her and that Baird was the better option for the party. 'The party needs me at the shit end,' Berejiklian told a close confidant.

Early the next morning, before the party room ballot, Berejiklian broke the news to her chief of staff that she was not contesting the leadership, and had agreed with

Baird that together they form a unity ticket. She would be his deputy. Others had toyed with putting their hand up for the premiership, including former sex discrimination commissioner Pru Goward and the right wing's favoured candidate, Anthony Roberts. Both pulled out and threw their support behind the Baird/Berejiklian unity ticket.

Baird was elected unopposed as premier and Berejiklian as deputy Liberal leader. The assumption was that Berejiklian would take over as treasurer, which would have been the obvious next step for her and a clear promotion. Instead, she told her staff that she wanted to remain in transport until the 2015 election and work her way through the final projects on that handwritten note she had given to McGrath several years earlier. Despite surrendering the job of her dreams, Berejiklian had a spring in her step and no one could work out why.

Baird has never divulged what conversations took place, including whether he and Berejiklian had a Kirribilli-style agreement, similar to the one between Bob Hawke and Paul Keating back in 1988. (Hawke and Keating had held a secret meeting at the prime minister's Sydney residence, where the pair forged a deal based on Keating later assuming the leadership.) Kean, among others, had always suspected that Baird told Berejiklian that he would serve for three years and then hand over the reins. Little else would explain her enthusiasm and upbeat attitude after missing out on the top job. 'I think at the time she thought the Right would tear her down, which goes way back to her preselection,' said Kean. 'I was devastated because she had the support to be premier, but looking back, she was right. She was able to send the message that she put the party first, before her personal ambition. Even when it came to being premier, she still thought about the Liberal Party before herself.' As for O'Farrell, in the days after his resignation he left no one in any doubt about how much he disapproved of Baird succeeding him.

Later in the year, just 10 days before Christmas in 2014, as Berejiklian's office was frantically trying to finalise the deal for the CBD light rail as well as shut down the Newcastle heavy rail to make way for the regional city's own tram, the unthinkable happened in Sydney. Mon Haron Monis, an Islamic-inspired terrorist, took hostages in the Lindt Cafe in Martin Place. The 17-hour siege paralysed the city and ended tragically. Two people were killed and three seriously injured. As the drama unfolded, panic ripped through the CBD as well as the government's office tower opposite the cafe.

Garbled messages were broadcast over the internal public announcement system, which only served to put more fear into the minds of ministers and their staff. At one stage, all ministers were told to leave their offices immediately and retreat to the safety of Baird's office, where extra police were on hand. Berejiklian refused to follow the order. She was not prepared to abandon her staff. When the building was finally evacuated through the fire exits, Berejiklian and McGrath were summoned to the state crisis centre, a secret war room located in a tower in Redfern. Security was so tight that only ministers and their chiefs of staff were allowed to know its exact location.

With the city in shutdown, Berejiklian's ministerial driver could not access the streets around Martin Place to pick them up. Instead, Berejiklian and McGrath walked out of the CBD. Berejiklian joined other key ministers, including Health Minister Brad Hazzard, in the crisis centre. Baird chaired the half-hourly meetings, and Prime Minister Tony Abbott and his chief of staff Peta Credlin dialled in on video hookups. Berejiklian's job was to get people home from the city, which had been brought to a complete standstill. She stayed at the crisis centre all through the night, working to get Sydney's transport system back on track.

Berejiklian was Baird's transport minister until the 2015 state election, which saw the Coalition comfortably returned despite losing seats to Labor. In Baird's new cabinet after the election, Berejiklian was appointed treasurer – the first female treasurer in New South Wales' history. The state's finances were in rude health and Berejiklian handed down two budgets that saw

New South Wales billions of dollars in the black. She continued as a loyal lieutenant to Baird as his star continued to rise. At one stage, opinion polls showed Baird was the most popular leader in the country, the golden boy who could do no wrong. But Magic Mike's fortunes took a dramatic skydive in the second half of 2016.

First, Baird took the extreme step of announcing that he would ban the whole greyhound industry after being horrified by a damning report into the industry and the number of dogs killed. His animal protection instincts turned out to be politically poisonous for the government. He also had a hugely unpopular policy to amalgamate local councils. Baird's council mergers and the greyhound ban cost the Coalition a seat in a by-election. He also had to contend with an anti-corruption commission inquiry involving 10 Liberal MPs accused of accepting money from banned donors before the 2011 state election. The former New South Wales parliamentary historian David Clune, who documented Macquarie Street for decades, said of Baird's demise: 'He fell off his tightrope dramatically. Progressives savaged him and conservatives felt betrayed.' By the time Christmas 2016 rolled around the government was in a funk, nonetheless there was no hint that Baird would pull up stumps. But Baird gave his future serious thought over the summer and met Berejiklian for breakfast on 19 January 2017 to tell her he was quitting politics.

Finally, it seemed, the premiership would be hers. She called Kean, who was out of town on a beach holiday, to ask him to shore up her support. Constance was Berejiklian's main threat to the top job, but planning minister Rob Stokes, who was in the UK studying his masters at Oxford at the time, was also a possible contender. Kean had one task: he had to guarantee the right wing of the party would back her in a leadership ballot. Kean called his mate Dominic Perrottet, the leader of the right. The pair were from opposing factions but had struck up a friendship back in their Young Liberal days. Kean told Perrottet that Berejiklian wanted him as her deputy leader and treasurer. The young and ambitious Perrottet jumped at the chance and promised that he would make sure his conservative colleagues were on board with Berejiklian becoming premier. The deal was done with one phone call, before Baird even publicly announced his resignation. Berejiklian was sworn in as New South Wales' 45th premier four days later.

Several months into Berejiklian's premiership, ballot papers for Australia's highly anticipated plebiscite on same sex marriage were turning up in people's letter-boxes across the country. It was September 2017 and Berejiklian was asked to speak at a New South Wales Parliament Says Yes fundraising event. The function was hosted by independent Sydney MP Alex Greenwich, a tireless campaigner for allowing same sex couples, which included him and his partner Victor, to marry in Australia. (The pair were married in Argentina, where same-sex marriage was legal, in 2012.) Greenwich was mentored by Sydney's longest-serving lord mayor Clover Moore and replaced her in state parliament when she was forced to choose between state politics and local government. The O'Farrell government had introduced the so-called 'get Clover' laws in 2012, which banned MPs from sitting on local councils, but essentially targeted the very popular Moore, a 24-year veteran of Macquarie Street.

When the invite to Greenwich's event landed in Berejiklian's in-tray, she accepted – but her staff told Greenwich not to expect much from the premier; she would turn up to his fundraiser and make a very brief statement. Instead, the supremely disciplined Berejiklian, who would never spontaneously go off script, delivered a considered, impassioned speech that Greenwich still considers one of the best he heard throughout the campaign. It was a turning point in the campaign, and their relationship.

Berejiklian had previously made it clear that she was a supporter of same sex marriage and had attended the launch of an event for Liberals and Nationals who were voting 'yes' in the postal plebiscite. But what stunned people at Greenwich's event was Berejiklian's conviction. 'I'm extremely proud to be here as premier of New South Wales. I am hoping that all of us will look back and feel really proud that we were part of something special, putting aside our political differences in support for what is one of the most important decisions of our time in terms of human rights and social justice,' Berejiklian told the crowd, which included senior members of her cabinet. 'For us it is a no-brainer, but for many in the community it won't be so simple. There's no doubt there are people with different religious views and faiths . . . that doesn't stop any of us from supporting what is right.'

Berejiklian's strong stance put her completely at odds with her Armenian Apostolic Church. The Armenian church in Sydney, where her parents had married, warned its congregation on its Facebook page just days later that their faith was 'under fire' by the postal survey. It said redefining marriage would have 'consequences' for religious freedom, free speech and children's education. The head of the Australia and New Zealand Diocese of the Armenian Church said his organisation respected gay people. 'We are against same sex marriage. We have nothing against gays and lesbians, nothing at all,' he said.

After Berejiklian's speech, Greenwich was back out campaigning early the next day, handing out 'yes' brochures in Sydney's busy Martin Place, when a woman approached him. She explained to Greenwich that she had a deep faith and had been adamant that she could not find it in her heart to support same sex marriage. Then she saw Berejiklian's comments from the night before reported in the media. Greenwich remembers the woman's words clearly: 'If Gladys can vote yes, I can vote yes.'

Greenwich maintains Berejiklian's role in the campaign cannot be underestimated. 'Her intervention was huge. She really knew the impact her words were going to have and her speech was incredibly powerful. She said it was a priority for Australia, she spoke about being a person of faith who supported it as the most important human rights issues of our times and there was no other Liberal leader who acknowledged the impact the plebiscite was having on the LGBTQI community.' Her speech at his event was a turning point for Greenwich. 'After she spoke that night, I developed a really strong respect for her. She knew how to communicate in a way that would have a positive impact and she was brave.'

Same sex marriage was not the only socially progressive issue that saw Berejiklian and Greenwich on the same page. One of Greenwich's key election platforms was lowering the rate of homelessness in Australia's largest city. In 2018, Greenwich slept rough and lived in boarding houses and crisis accommodation for 10 days as part of the SBS show *Filthy Rich and Homeless*. Berejiklian made a point of watching his episode.

The next year during the election campaign, Berejiklian took the unconventional step of asking Greenwich to be part of an announcement where the Liberals committed to an ambitious target to end homelessness in Sydney by 2030.

It was the first, and only, time Greenwich had been invited to stand with the government for an election promise – such opportunities were usually exclusively reserved for Coalition candidates. It further cemented Greenwich's respect for Berejiklian ahead of what would become the biggest, and most bitter, battle that they would embark on together. Greenwich, with Berejiklian's support and encouragement, would later work to bring New South Wales in line with the rest of the country and decriminalise abortion.

After two years as premier, on paper, Berejiklian should have had an easy path to victory in 2019. Her government was building train lines, tram tracks and schools. The state's finances were the strongest they had been in years, thanks to the sale of publicly owned electricity poles and wires, and her team was largely united. Liberal Party–commissioned focus groups showed voters saw Berejiklian as diligent, honest and dependable. The perfect head girl, as she came to be known in the media.

But there was one group of voters who did not care about the state election or Berejiklian: women aged 35 to 54 with children. Party strategists concluded that Berejiklian could not win the election if she failed to convince that very specific demographic to vote for her. There was genuine fear that the Coalition was facing an electoral loss.

The Liberal Party turned to Sydney marketing agency Drum Digital, which specialised in social media campaigns aimed at young and middle-aged mothers. The agency devised ads for Facebook. 'Too much screen time can hold back a child's development,' one post said, accompanied by a photo of a young girl glued to a device. 'That's why the NSW Liberals are doubling the Active Kids program to $200 a year.' (The program provided vouchers for school-aged kids to help cover the costs of playing weekend sport.) The Liberal Party sent two million mailouts, addressed only to the women they needed to target. Berejiklian told them her priority was to take pressure off families. One version of the targeted mail saw Berejiklian write to mums stressing that 'our families matter'. Her letters were handwritten and simply signed 'Gladys'.

While Berejiklian was struggling to win over mothers, one obvious advantage she had in the lead up to the 2019 election was that the Labor Party had sensationally lost its leader Luke Foley just months earlier. Berejiklian's Liberal cabinet minister David Elliott used the cover of parliamentary privilege to throw mud at the Opposition leader. Elliott, the government's go-to bomb thrower, did not name anyone when he said to Foley: 'I haven't had a little bit too much to drink at a party and harassed an ABC journalist. I've never done that.' Foley denied the accusation, but Elliott's words delivered the desired damage.

Caught in the crossfire was the journalist, ABC TV reporter Ashleigh Raper, who against her wishes was forced to publicly address claims that Foley had inappropriately touched her. When Foley later reneged on a promise to her that he would resign, Raper released a public statement. She lambasted politicians for using females as political footballs and said women should be able to go about their professional lives and socialise without being subjected to inexcusable behaviour by men. Just days after the release of her statement, Berejiklian called Raper to check how she was faring and to offer her support. It was a very kind gesture, according to Raper, despite Berejiklian's own people playing a role in the saga to ensure the downfall of an opponent. Experienced Labor MP Michael Daley, who had been a minister when Labor was last in power, replaced Foley as leader just four months before the election.

At one point during the campaign, the marginal seat of Penrith in Sydney's west, held by sports minister Stuart Ayres, reached its break-glass moment for the Liberals. Ayres' colleagues were seriously worried about his prospects if there was a backlash from voters over his handling of the government's decision to rebuild the Sydney Football Stadium in the eastern suburbs. The stadiums issue had been a thorn in the side of the Liberal's election campaign. Labor had seized on it as its only issue, arguing that schools and hospitals would be neglected because the government was wasting money on rebuilding sporting stadiums in inner Sydney. John Howard was called in to help. As it is written in Liberal lore: if in doubt, roll Howard out. Howard was treated like a celebrity.

Influential radio broadcaster and Liberal heavyweight Alan Jones helped break the back of Daley's campaign with the two memorably clashing over Labor's opposition to the football stadium's rebuilding. Only months earlier, Jones also had a fiery exchange with the chief executive of the Sydney Opera House, Louise Herron, over her opposition to parts of a plan to project the barrier draw of Sydney's richest horse race The Everest on the sails of the city's most iconic building. Jones thundered on air that Herron should be sacked (he later apologised for his behaviour after coming under fire for his inappropriate comments). In an interview with the *Sydney Morning Herald*, long-time political observer Deborah Snow asked Berejiklian if she was scared of Jones. 'I'm not scared of anybody,' she replied. 'If I was scared of anybody I wouldn't be in this job.'

But one disastrous day during the election campaign, Berejiklian was uncharacteristically rattled as she made a concerted effort not to even utter the word 'stadium' at the daily press conference. One of her most senior advisers had convinced her that she could draw attention away from the issue that was causing a headache for her government if she pretended the stadiums imbroglio did not exist. The advice to not say the s-word was ill-thought. It only served to further highlight the issue.

In a crisis meeting to work out their next step, her strategy team threw around some options. One idea was to wind back the city's controversial lockout laws, which saw strict rules imposed on drinking venues in a bid to reduce alcohol-fuelled violence. A side effect of the restrictive laws saw life being sucked out of parts of Sydney. Or, as a distraction, perhaps Berejiklian could announce that the Coalition would decriminalise abortion. Abortion was hardly going to be an election-winning issue, not least because the right-wing religious element of her parliamentary party would lose their minds. Both suggestions were swiftly dismissed and Berejiklian changed tack on stadiums. The next day, she got her mojo back and held a feisty press conference insisting that her government had managed the economy so well that voters could have it all: stadiums *and* billions of dollars worth of services and other infrastructure. Party strategists breathed a huge sigh of relief.

Just eight days out from the state election, a terrorist attack at the hands of an Australian man devastated the New Zealand city of Christchurch. Brenton Tarrant, who grew up in the New South Wales town of Grafton, killed 51 people in a shooting rampage at two Muslim mosques. Shocked by the killings, Berejiklian wanted to visit a mosque in Lakemba in Sydney's west to pay her respects. One of her closest advisers, Ehssan Veiszadeh, was a practising Muslim and Berejiklian knew how difficult the killings had been for him and his family. But her security detail would not give her clearance to go to the mosque. They had some concerning intelligence about some young Muslim men who were speaking at an event nearby. Berejiklian was undeterred. She told her security that she didn't want them to accompany her if they did not feel safe, but she would be going regardless. And she did.

In Liberal Party headquarters, a group of political appa-ratchiks worked in the aptly named dirt unit, designed to do exactly what its informal title suggests – dig dirt on their opponents and pressure journalists who wrote stories they did not agree with, or were from publica-tions they did not like. The *Daily Telegraph* was the Liberals' paper of choice for the dissemination of the dirt. Heading up the dirt unit at the time was sitting upper house Liberal MP Peter Phelps, who through some basic googling and YouTube trawling stumbled across gold. Without too much trouble, he found a video of Daley at a politics in the pub event claiming that young people were leaving Sydney and being replaced by Asians with PhDs. 'Moving in and taking their jobs', was Daley's line. The story was handed to the *Telegraph*, which posted it online in time for the commercial television stations to cover it in their 6 pm bulletins, and other publications to also run the story.

Berejiklian was personally affronted by Daley's com-ments. Apart from being an own goal for Labor – which was the turning point in the election campaign – it went to the very heart of Berejiklian's being, with the comments resembling the anti-Asian sentiment she had protested against as Young Liberal president in the 1990s. As Daley's comments made national headlines and forced Labor into serious damage control, Berejiklian texted Jenny Leong, Greens MP for the inner Sydney seat of Newtown, and the first woman of Chinese Australian heritage to be elected to a lower house seat in Australia. Berejiklian's message to Leong was very clear: she would never tolerate any racism in her government. Leong appreciated Berejiklian's empathy and goodwill towards her.

Leong and Berejiklian's politics made them the most unlikely allies in the parliament but both had a healthy respect for each other through their shared migrant backgrounds. Leong tells the story of her and Berejiklian turning up to parliament one day wearing the same suit from Australian designer Cue (Leong only wears ethical clothing made in Australia and Cue fits that bill). The moment when they realised they matched was captured by photographers, and shows them both laughing like schoolgirls at the fashion faux pas. Berejiklian promised Leong she would not wear that outfit to parliament again; she acknowledged that her position meant she had a more extensive suit wardrobe than the Greens MP. Leong says it was another example of Berejiklian's generosity towards her.

After Daley's 'Asians with PhDs' comments emerged, the Labor leader never regained his composure. Berejiklian, on the other hand, stayed disciplined and on message. In the final days of the campaign, Berejiklian and Daley faced off in one of only two televised leaders' debates. The Liberals chose Sky News as the host for the final debate. Daley made a spectacular blunder when he could not put a dollar figure on the state's education budget. Berejiklian's performance, while not flawless, showed her undeniable ability to be across detail. Her days of high school debating paid off. She knew her stuff and ran rings around her opponent. Berejiklian was within striking distance of victory.

Three days later, Berejiklian was triumphant, although her election win was not a resounding result. As polls closed on election day, but before counting had even begun, Berejiklian phoned Greenwich – who was enjoying a glass of wine at his Kings Cross apartment after a day on the voting booths – to stress how keen she was to work with him if the Coalition won. The three independent MPs were going to be crucial to Berejiklian in navigating minority government, and she needed them on side from the very beginning.

Wearing one of her favourite Australian designers – Karen Gee – Berejiklian was on stage at the Liberal election party at the Sofitel Wentworth by 10 pm. She had deliberately chosen to wear pink as a colour synonymous with women. To a rapturous crowd, which included party heavyweights like Howard, O'Farrell and Greiner, an ecstatic Berejiklian thanked her parents and sisters, before declaring: 'What is most important to me is that, no matter what your background – where you live, what your circumstances – everybody in this state has the chance to be their best. A state in which someone with a long surname – and a woman – can be the premier of New South Wales.' Liberal moderate powerbroker, lobbyist and one-time New South Wales minister Michael Photios declared that 'a young Armenian Australian from Ryde has emerged a Labor dragon slayer' and the *Sunday Telegraph* dubbed her 'Gladiator'.

Berejiklian had made history. She was the first popularly elected female premier in New South Wales, and at last she had a mandate to do things her way.

5

HER NUMERO UNO

THE MAN BEREJIKLIAN EVENTUALLY FELL FOR WAS 11 years her senior and had earned himself the nickname Dodgy Daryl in the halls of Macquarie Street well before his failed business ventures were uncovered and he was outed as Berejiklian's secret love. Daryl Maguire's colleagues used to joke that the member for Wagga Wagga was always selling 'trinkets from China' from his Parliament House office and had a reputation for being a small-time wheeler and dealer. But not everyone saw Maguire in that light. He was a highly respected figure in Wagga Wagga. His friend of more than 30 years, the former deputy prime minister Michael McCormack, insists that when it came to his electorate, Maguire's heart was in the right place. 'Daryl will have the word "disgraced" in front of his name forever more and that is a shame,' McCormack reflected. 'He was a good local member, he got stuff done. There would not be anyone else in Wagga with as many plaques with their name on them as Daryl Maguire.'

Maguire was an accidental MP. He was active in the Wagga Wagga chamber of commerce and a Liberal Party member, but he was never destined for a career in politics. Rather, the very popular Wagga Wagga lawyer Anthony Paul was always in line to replace the long-serving Liberal MP Joe Schipp when he retired from New South Wales parliament. McCormack said Paul was a pillar of society. 'Anthony was a leading solicitor in town, he was branch president of the Liberal Party, he was the bloke who would turn up to the school charity fete and he would be on the back of the ute turning the chocolate wheel and calling out the numbers,' McCormack said. 'Everyone knew and everyone loved Anthony but he made one big mistake. Anthony didn't go to all the branches because he thought the seat was his to take, he thought it was a fait accompli.'

Maguire, on the other hand, made a point of getting to know the smallest of branches in outlying towns. He turned up to their meetings, no matter the size, and addressed the members. 'He smooched up to the Wagga women's branch, which is probably the biggest women's branch in the New South Wales division,' McCormack said.

'And lo and behold, he beat Anthony Paul by one vote.' Against the odds, Maguire was preselected for the safe seat and was elected to parliament in 1999. In his maiden speech, he described Wagga Wagga as the 'centre of the universe'. He was 'captivated by its beauty, blinded by its potential and passionate for its cause and its people'.

Maguire boasted that he was one of few Australian politicians with Indian heritage. In an interview with SBS Punjabi, Maguire played up his multicultural background. 'I have actually had some research done and there aren't too many that can claim to have Indian heritage, as parliamentarians. There are several English people that were born in India that served in the parliament, but not many that had an Indian grandfather. So I think that that's one for the board, one to chalk up,' he told SBS radio host Manpreet Kaur Singh, who made a joke about them sharing a surname. Maguire's great-grandfather, Sunda Singh, was a Sikh hawker from Punjab who moved to Australia in the late 1800s. Singh married an English woman and bought a dairy farm and a general store, and he was one of the first to own a car in Swan Hill, regional Victoria, according to Maguire.

Maguire's early years were marred by tragedy and he used his maiden speech to parliament to describe his humble beginnings. He was brought up by his young, widowed father, a stockman who could barely write his own name but ensured his two children received an education.

Maguire told the story of him and his sister having to travel '100 miles to school each day, rain, hail or shine, on dirt and muddy roads'. Maguire started his working life as an apprentice car mechanic in Griffith before moving on to run homewares and electrical stores in the Riverina. He married Maureen and had two children, James and Kara. But his big break came when he took over the Wagga Wagga franchise of Harvey Norman.

His later business ventures may have been flops but Maguire, by all accounts, did have a talent for selling whitegoods. Harvey Norman boss Gerry Harvey remembers Maguire as skilled in self-promotion. 'You talk about quality in sales people and you give him a mark out of 10, it would have been about eight, eight and a half. He was way above average,' Harvey told *The Weekend Australian Magazine* late in 2021. 'Some people love being the centre of attention and they like doing their own ads and people recognise them, and he was very, very good at that.' In another interview, the retail king described Maguire as 'a good salesman, a good franchisee and he made reasonably good money at the time. He left of his own accord because he wanted to go into politics. Now he's worth no money, has completely ruined himself and is just a tragic figure.'

Maguire spent his first 12 years in parliament as a little-known country backbencher while the Labor Party, led by Bob Carr, reigned in New South Wales. However, in 2011, after 16 years languishing in Opposition, the Liberals and Nationals were back in power following Labor's landslide loss with Kristina Keneally as leader. Maguire, who for more than a decade in Macquarie Street had little pull or friends in high places, suddenly found he had much more sway to deliver for Wagga Wagga. While Berejiklian embarked on her new role as transport minister, Premier Barry O'Farrell gave Maguire the plum position of whip, which comes with extra pay and kudos, and he was made chair of the NSW Parliament Asia-Pacific Friendship Group.

Maguire was also appointed a parliamentary secretary, but never managed to secure the keys to a ministry. His colleagues say Maguire had few close mates in the 20 years he was in Macquarie Street, other than O'Farrell and upper house MP and left-wing powerbroker Don Harwin, who was also elected to parliament in 1999 and was one of Berejiklian's allies. Maguire also had a reputation for being over-friendly with some male colleagues. Senior cabinet minister Rob Stokes said Maguire used to pinch him on the backside while Matt Kean remembers receiving text messages from Maguire when he first entered parliament commenting on the much younger Kean's looks. A male newspaper editor recalls Maguire starting phone conversations with, 'Hello handsome'.

If Maguire had a low profile in state politics, that suddenly, and spectacularly, changed in July 2018, when he became entangled in a corruption inquiry into the former Canterbury City Council, in Sydney's inner west – a local government area at least 400 kilometres from Maguire's home town of Wagga Wagga. The ICAC was looking into a property development scandal involving a former Liberal councillor and associate of Maguire who was accused of dishonestly exercising his public functions.

When it comes to property development scandals in councils, New South Wales has a long and lurid history. The ICAC has investigated many since its inception in 1988, when the Liberal government established an integrity commission on the back of 'halfhearted and cosmetic approaches to preventing public sector corruption', as Nick Greiner told parliament at the time. In the ultimate irony, only four years later the very commission that Greiner set up ended his political career. Greiner was forced to stand down as premier in 1992 after the commission handed down adverse findings against him. Greiner was accused of misusing his position as Liberal Party leader to secure Liberal-turned-independent MP Terry Metherell's resignation from state parliament to achieve political advantage. Greiner offered Metherell a position with a government agency in order to prompt a by-election, which the Liberals would likely win. Greiner was ultimately cleared by the New South Wales Court of Appeal but his political career was over.

Even back then, dubious Liberals dubbed the ICAC 'Frankenstein's monster'.

Greiner, who established the anti-corruption commission on the back of a 1988 election promise, has since been convinced that the model he devised is flawed (perhaps, in part, because it has not yet claimed a Labor premier). His view, nearly 35 years after he set it up, is that the ICAC has too much power and is too slow to make decisions. It was also a mistake to include mandatory public hearings in the ICAC structure, he told the *Australian Financial Review* soon after Berejiklian's resignation. He said: 'I think integrity of government is fashionable in New South Wales at the moment with the Gladys situation. I think we probably got some of the elements of ICAC wrong, though.'

Among the long list of property development scandals to land before the ICAC, one of the most colourful and salacious scandals remains the love triangle that enveloped Wollongong City Council, south of Sydney, in the mid 2000s. The ICAC heard that a council town planner was sleeping with three developers and accepting perfume, cash, handbags, housing renovations and holidays from them while assessing their development applications.

The Canterbury City Council ICAC inquiry in 2018 was less lascivious than the Wollongong probe but just as damaging. On day 24 of the hearing – Friday 13 July –

a secret phone recording was played where Maguire was heard talking about organising a 'quick sale' for a 'mega-big client'. It was an extraordinary revelation: a sitting MP with a side hustle that involved brokering multimillion-dollar property deals for commission. Maguire had called his Canterbury councillor associate Michael Hawatt on 9 May 2016, soon after they had both returned from trips to China. Unbeknown to either of them, the call was being recorded by ICAC investigators. Maguire, then a parliamentary secretary for the centenary of Anzac, counter terrorism, corrections and veterans, asked Hawatt for any shovel-ready sites in Canterbury for his client.

'My client is mega-big and has got mega money and wants two or three development application–approved projects right now. Today,' Maguire told his Liberal councillor mate. The 'mega-big' client Maguire was referring to was the Australian arm of the major Chinese property developer Country Garden. Hong Kong–listed Country Garden is one of the largest Chinese apartment developers when measured by sales.

The ICAC uncovered Maguire talking extensively about business prospects with Hawatt. In another phone tap, Maguire told his friend: 'I've got half a dozen people that are always seeking stuff.' Country Garden could put Maguire on retainer and pay him a 'couple of grand a day', the MP was recorded telling Hawatt. And even if Country Garden was not interested in projects, there were others about. 'I've got the Malaysians,' Maguire boasted.

The evidence was damning, and Maguire conceded to the ICAC that he was in fact trying to pursue a 'money-making exercise', although his efforts came to nothing. 'I believe it was the intent,' Maguire told the ICAC when asked whether the goal was for him and Hawatt to share commissions on property deals. When the ICAC handed down its report into the Canterbury scandal in March 2021, Hawatt was found to have engaged in 'serious corrupt conduct'. The ICAC also said it would seek legal advice as to whether Maguire should be charged with 'giving false or misleading evidence to an inquiry'. That offence can carry up to five years in jail.

McCormack says he was 'gobsmacked' when the first corruption allegations against Maguire emerged. Maguire was 'always wheeling and dealing, but you never thought it was in a bad way'. McCormack, by then deputy prime minister, vividly remembers landing in South Australia as the allegations were emerging. McCormack's phone 'went crazy' once he was on the tarmac. 'I was floored,' he recalls. McCormack had known Maguire since the 1980s, first when McCormack was the editor of Wagga Wagga's local paper *The Daily Advertiser* and then later when he pursued a federal political career. 'There were very few days when Daryl and I didn't talk, we were very close,' McCormack said. 'I have never had a sleepless night in politics, but I lay in bed that night and wondered why, I just couldn't believe it.'

Respected former Nationals MP Kay Hull was just as shocked. Hull had also known Maguire for many years and held the federal seat of Riverina for 12 years before McCormack. Like her successor, Hull was resolute that Maguire was a very good local member. 'Daryl Maguire did what any local member should do and that is to deliver for the electorate,' Hull said. 'Sure, he may have been aggressive, but sometimes you have to be to be heard. Yes, he may have been bullish but so be it. He delivered for his community.' The regional city had desperately needed a new hospital since the 1970s, but that only happened once Maguire pushed for it. Wagga Wagga, she said, would not have a new ambulance station or modern courthouse without Maguire's representation. 'I do not condone for a second the activities that he has admitted to but I will never criticise Daryl's work as a local member.'

His achievements no longer mattered. Maguire's political career was over as soon as his name was mentioned in the Canterbury City Council ICAC investigation. Not that he was prepared to accept it. Outside the ICAC in Sydney's CBD, Maguire apologised for causing 'embarrassment and disappointment to a lot of people'. Hours after his stunning ICAC appearance in July 2018, he resigned as parliamentary secretary and quit the New

South Wales Liberal Party. Berejiklian was on leave and the New South Wales Nationals leader John Barilaro was acting premier.

Barilaro accepted Maguire's resignation. 'Daryl told the truth, he's admitted that he's done wrong and he's now paying that price,' Barilaro said. 'I'm very disappointed. That's why in this state, this government has put in place the toughest legislation when it comes to corruption, something that we've worked very hard for to give confidence to the people of New South Wales that we would stamp out corruption.' Despite Barilaro's tough words, Maguire was determined to stay in parliament as the independent member for Wagga Wagga. He faced an unrelenting weekend of pressure from colleagues, the Labor Party and Wagga Wagga mayor Greg Conkey who, despite knowing Maguire for 30 years, saw his position as untenable. Maguire refused to budge.

Berejiklian was forced to weigh in. Despite being on holiday, she released a statement urging her colleague (and secret lover) to reconsider, pointing out that he had let down the voters in Wagga Wagga. Defiant, Maguire recorded a video message for his Facebook page where he apologised for breaching the code of conduct for parliamentary secretaries but vowed to stay on until the March 2019 election. 'I've removed myself from the Liberal Party. I've resigned from the party only, but I won't resign as a member of parliament.' His stance lasted a little over a week. At Berejiklian's urging, Maguire's long-time friend O'Farrell was called on to intervene and the former premier managed to convince Maguire that he had to quit parliament.

Maguire's resignation forced a by-election in his ultra-safe Liberal seat, which the party had held for almost six decades. Hull was being urged to run. Although it had never been a consideration for her, she was forced to give it some serious thought when the National Party begged her to be its candidate. Internal party research showed only Hull could win the seat. Berejiklian was also anxious to know her plans, acutely aware that Hull's popularity could see the Liberals surrender the seat to the Nationals. Regardless of the polling, the Liberals were determined to keep their hold on Wagga Wagga without their junior Coalition colleague getting in their way. Eventually the Nationals caved in, but not before Barilaro threatened to quit as leader of his party if they pushed ahead with contesting the seat, citing the need for Coalition unity. The Liberals selected inexperienced Snowy Valleys councillor Julia Ham – Berejiklian's choice.

Berejiklian managed expectations from the start, warning that it would be a tough ask for voters to forgive her government after Maguire's actions. The timing was also disastrous because Wagga Wagga went to the polls just one month after a bruising period of infighting between the federal Liberals in Canberra, which brutally ended Malcolm Turnbull's leadership and saw him replaced by Scott Morrison as prime minister. Berejiklian made a handful of trips to the Riverina during the by-election campaign, promising more than $100 million on a range of projects in Wagga Wagga, including $10 million for the Riverina Conservatorium of Music. At the time, one Liberal said: 'With the money being spent in Wagga, you should be able to get a donkey up.' One of her most senior ministers could not fathom why Berejiklian was willing to tie herself to a seat that was surely going to be lost. 'I just could not understand why she kept going down there, to fight a by-election that was brought on by a bloke who was before ICAC.'

Even with a healthy dose of pork-barrelling and a constant parade of ministers through Wagga Wagga, Berejiklian's hand-picked candidate could not hold the seat and the Liberals suffered a crushing defeat to local doctor Joe McGirr, who ran as an independent. The swing away from the Liberals was almost 30 per cent. It was a humiliating outcome for the government. Late on the Saturday night, after the by-election result was clear, Berejiklian called members of the New South Wales press gallery to brief them on what had gone wrong. She pointed the finger at her federal colleagues. Her then–secret partner's misdemeanours had brought on the by-election, but she believed the civil war in Canberra had ultimately cost her a blue-ribbon seat.

Maguire first came to the attention of ICAC investigators during the Canterbury City Council inquiry, but his role in advancing the business interests of a number of Chinese-born associates, as well as allegations he misused his public office and parliamentary resources to enrich himself, meant that by September 2020, he was the subject of a new inquiry – and this time he was centre stage. Codenamed Operation Keppel, the inquiry was set down for four weeks and its announcement took few by surprise, given Maguire's revelations at the earlier council inquiry, although no one knew what was coming, or who would ultimately be caught up in his web of dodgy business dealings.

Wagga Wagga may have been the centre of his world, but Maguire had a very strong and long-running interest in China. In August 1995, Maguire – who at the time was Wagga Wagga's chamber of commerce president – was part of an eight-member delegation who travelled to Kunming, Wagga Wagga's sister city, for its well-known export commodities fair. The favour was returned the following year when Maguire invited his counterpart, the president of the Kunming chamber of commerce, to visit Wagga Wagga. Over the following four years, before becoming an MP, Maguire was involved with at least two more official Chinese visits to the Riverina.

Then, during his years as the local member, Maguire made many more trips, so much so that he was dubbed

Mr China by some of his parliamentary colleagues. In August 2002, Maguire flew to China for 11 days, with some of his trip paid for by Sydney-based ACA Capital Investments. Over the next decade, Maguire had dealings with ACA Capital's director Humphrey Xu, who was later named as the businessman who was allegedly pressured by Chinese spy agencies to cultivate senior federal Labor MPs.

McCormack admitted he found it a little strange that Maguire was always travelling to China but never thought there was anything untoward. One of Maguire's big money-making ideas was to build a textiles manufacturing warehouse in Wagga Wagga (coincidentally in the same street as the city's gun club, which would later come to the attention of the ICAC), with the help of his Chinese connections. 'It was going to be the be-all and end-all but it just never got off the ground. But that was Daryl, always talking big,' McCormack said.

As part of its investigations into Maguire, the ICAC tendered his itinerary for a jam-packed trip in July 2012 to Hangzhou, where Maguire planned to visit a university, the massive Wu Ai Market in Shenyang (which sells everything from clothes and shoes to Christmas decorations and Chinese trinkets), and the Great Wall and the Forbidden City in Beijing. The trip was part of Maguire's push to get a $400 million Chinese trade centre for Wagga Wagga. In December that year, the city's council signed a memorandum of understanding with the Chinese state-owned Wuai Group and Xu's ACA Capital Investments after the council offered to sell some land for the centre. O'Farrell, as premier, and Maguire were there for the signing but the deal ultimately collapsed, with a council report citing community concern over a 'lack of transparency'.

On another trip to China in November 2015, Maguire visited the headquarters of property developers Aoyuan International – a curious meeting because the company had never proposed any developments for the Riverina. Nonetheless Maguire secured a meeting with the company's chairman Guo Zi Wen at its headquarters in Guangzhou in southern China. Maguire flaunted his political connections, boasting to investors and government colleagues that he had met Chinese President Xi Jinping. Turns out that he did indeed 'meet' Xi, along with 15 other MPs who lined up to greet the president during his visit to Sydney in 2014. Berejiklian, then transport minister, was photographed standing behind Maguire at that meet and greet.

In his opening submission to Operation Keppel in September 2020, counsel assisting the ICAC Scott Robertson said he would argue that Maguire 'improperly used his role and the diplomatic weight of his office as chair of the Asia-Pacific Friendship Group as a door opener or gateway in the pursuit of his own financial interests and private Chinese business interests'. Two intercepted phone calls kicked off proceedings, where Maguire was heard doing exactly that: spruiking his connections in the Asia-Pacific region, with it later emerging that Maguire had his sights on helping his business associates set up a casino in Samoa. But the ICAC probe was to be centred around a company called G8way International Pty Ltd, of which Maguire was moonlighting as a silent director while a member of parliament.

G8way International claimed to offer an immigration service, business network and chaperoned travel, with influence and experience that 'reaches to high levels of government'. With fees starting as low as $500 a year, G8way International could provide vital connections needed to source products in Asia, especially milk and cotton. It could also explore financial interests in property developments from southwest Sydney to the Gold Coast. But what G8way International really specialised in was immigration. While his colleagues may have joked he was selling Chinese wares from his parliamentary office, the reality was Maguire was using his office as the part-time headquarters for a private business network with a focus on a cash-for-visa scheme for rich families in China.

Maguire's foot soldier was a migrant agent called Maggie Wang, who attended at least half a dozen meetings in Parliament House to hand Maguire up to $20,000 cash in envelopes. Wang and Maguire agreed in 2013 to set up their migration scheme to secure visas for about a dozen Chinese nationals. Employers were only obliged to keep an applicant on their books for three months, with all wages and superannuation covered by the Chinese applicant. The visa applicants were charged a fee split between Wang, Maguire and a regional business, which pocketed kickbacks worth about $30,000. Payments were always made in cash to avoid a paper trail, and Wang delivered Maguire's fee to him in person, handing over wads of notes. Asked why she was paid less than Maguire when she did a lot of the heavy lifting to make the scheme work, Wang said: 'The biggest part is to get the businesses to agree.'

Maguire's role was to identify the businesses, mostly around Wagga Wagga, to take part in the scheme. In one instance, the ICAC heard that vigneron Gerry McCormick, owner of Cottontails Winery in the Riverina, helped secure a visa for a Chinese national in exchange for selling his wine in China. McCormick received tens of thousands of dollars in cash for taking part in the scheme and was reimbursed for wages for a worker who never turned up.

Another Wagga Wagga businessman, real estate agent Angus McLaren, told the ICAC that Wang pitched a 'pretty good deal' to him. He only began to become suspicious when one of the workers he was expecting did not turn up, despite McLaren being handed wads of cash.

McLaren told the ICAC that he called Maguire for reassurance. 'I said what's going on here – we're getting paid in cash,' he said. '[Maguire] said, "I don't want to know about it" and changed the subject.'

'You've been introduced to this person [Wang] by a Member of Parliament and, naively, you thought it was a legitimate scheme,' McLaren told the ICAC. 'But when the cash started turning up I realised it wasn't.' He eventually concluded it was a 'dead set' scam.

McLaren told the ICAC, 'I didn't have an epiphany that this was a scam, it was a gradual realisation . . . But at that stage I thought we'd already crossed the Rubicon, so what do you do?'

Wine, steel, cotton and milk powder were some of the other failed ventures Maguire explored through the business, as well as an aeroplane pilot school, a trade showroom in China, a coal mine, a gold mine, a tin mine and even an automatic car wash. The self-confessed door opener was pinning his hopes on G8way International to set him up for retirement post-politics and help pay off some of the significant debts he had racked up, including as part of his divorce from his wife of many years, Maureen.

By 2017, when Berejiklian was premier, her office had to intervene to stop Maguire from visiting Shanghai on an urgent business trip that would have coincided with a ministerial trade mission. Maguire had written what was described as an 'appalling and provocative' letter to a Chinese conglomerate after it attempted to exit a joint venture with an oaten hay company with which he had financial ties. Maguire wrote that Australian governments would reconsider future joint ventures with Chinese companies over the issue, which was causing 'loss of face' for his political leaders. Berejiklian's chief of staff Sarah Cruickshank described the letter as 'ridiculous'. She told the ICAC: 'We've got this random MP proposing to fly to China before we go on an official trade mission. The simple reality is not even the minister of trade or the premier would write a letter in that tone.'

Maguire's cash-for-visas scheme was not his only attempt to cook up a money spinner. While an MP, Maguire stood to earn almost $1 million if he could help in the sale of a block of land at Badgerys Creek near Western Sydney Airport on behalf of racing heir Louise Raedler Waterhouse. Maguire agreed to help iron out road and zoning issues by speaking to authorities for Waterhouse and her property agent. Chinese investment broker and property agent William Luong told the anti-corruption commission that he gave Waterhouse a proposed consultancy agreement for the sale of the land with a service fee on a 'sliding scale'. The land lay within a stone's throw of the new airport and was expected to fetch between $330 and $360 million. At one point, Maguire gave Waterhouse Berejiklian's private email address, urging Waterhouse to contact the premier who would be able to provide a 'tickle from the top'. Waterhouse was not accused of any wrongdoing.

The witness list for Operation Keppel was long and varied, and it included other business associates such as Shanghai-born Jimmy Liu, whose agribusiness company United World Enterprises paid for Maguire to travel to China. On one occasion, Liu wrote a $1400 cheque for Maguire so that he could pay off his credit card. A parliamentary colleague, Liberal MP Mark Coure, also appeared and told the ICAC that Maguire never had permission to use his position as chair of the parliament's Asia-Pacific Friendship Group to link his Chinese business associates with oil companies in Australia.

On another occasion, in November 2017, Liberal Party donor and property developer Joseph Alha told the ICAC he was 'a bit tipsy' when he visited Berejiklian's office, after months of trying to salvage an ailing development project. Alha said he had been drinking in Maguire's Parliament House office for about three hours when the two men ventured to Berejiklian's office. They had already shared office drinks that afternoon with the chief of staff to the then Planning Minister Anthony Roberts.

Maguire had already told the developer in an intercepted phone call, 'We might have some drinks in my office and you never know who drops in.' In another call, Alha told Maguire: 'I think I should be privileged to one appointment . . . with Anthony Roberts and Gladys.' ICAC surveillance photographs showed Alha arriving at Macquarie Street with a large box containing a model of one of his developments.

Maguire was quick to point out that he would not have allowed Alha to take his wine with him. 'I wouldn't let anyone walk around parliament with a glass of red. I would frown on that.'

Mountains of remarkable evidence emerged during the ICAC's inquiry into Maguire, but nothing would compare to the appearance of Berejiklian on 12 October 2020. Her colleagues were relaxed about Berejiklian being on the witness list. The joke was that Berejiklian was so clean, she would be more likely to be embroiled in a sex scandal than a corruption scandal. No one could work out which of those propositions would be more ludicrous. Everyone – her colleagues, the Opposition and the media – expected a very uneventful appearance from the premier.

Her close confidant Matt Kean was in the wilderness between Armidale and Kempsey in northern New South Wales, with the then agriculture minister Adam Marshall and the former water minister Melinda Pavey, to announce a pumped hydro project. Berejiklian spoke to Kean at 8.30 am on the day of her ICAC appearance. She was flustered and told him something 'embarrassing' was going to emerge. Berejiklian asked him to keep an eye on colleagues, and singled out Stuart Ayres, who she was convinced could try to destabilise her leadership. Kean was blasé. He joked that the anti-corruption commission wouldn't come after her for stealing a paperclip.

Kean was out of mobile phone range for the rest of the morning and had no idea what was unfolding in Sydney. Other than a select few in her office who had been briefed on what to expect so they could prepare a strategy, no one else knew what was coming. After more than three weeks of public hearings before the corruption inquiry into Maguire, the Berejiklian bombshell came in the form of a simple question. 'Ms Berejiklian, have you ever been in a close personal relationship with Mr Maguire?' Robertson asked. Her response was simply: 'That's correct.'

Stunned colleagues hurriedly tuned in to the web stream to watch her evidence. The ICAC would not usually livestream its inquiries, but the pandemic prevented its hearings from being open to the public. Had it not been for the health restrictions, very few people would have witnessed the awkward moment when Berejiklian had to tell the ICAC that she had been in a close personal relationship with Maguire since the 2015 state election. She only ended contact with him a month before giving evidence. 'I would like to say at the outset that Mr Maguire was a colleague of 15 years, he was someone that I trusted . . . and that developed into a close personal relationship,' adding that their relationship was kept secret because she is a 'very private person'.

'We were close,' she said. It took a few minutes for the penny to drop, and for the term 'close personal relationship' to be understood by those watching her evidence unfold. In a devastating development, Berejiklian had been in a romantic relationship with the most unlikely man.

Despite having to sack him, Berejiklian conceded that she didn't cut off contact with Maguire until she was required to give evidence in a secret ICAC hearing in August 2020 and became aware of the nature of the allegations against him. 'When I was asked to support this inquiry, it became apparent to me that I should have absolutely no contact anymore with that individual.' It was also not clear how long the romance had been going on. Berejiklian said five years; Maguire said it was an on-again, off-again relationship, throwing around dates from 2013 to 2016 during his evidence. The ICAC revealed a text message showing Maguire using the Armenian term of endearment *hawkiss* for Berejiklian in 2014. 'Hawkiss good news. One of my contacts sold a motel for 5.8 million. I had put her in contact so I should make 5k,' Maguire's message said. 'Congrats!!! Great news!!! Woohoo,' Berejiklian responded.

The trail of evidence would have been humiliating for Berejiklian. Revelations also came that she attended meetings, functions and dinners also attended by Maguire's secret business partners and associates. One itinerary tabled as evidence showed that, just weeks after becoming premier, Berejiklian travelled to Wagga Wagga on a formal visit and attended a private dinner at Maguire's house with his business partner Phil Elliott and Elliot's spouse.

But surveillance of phone calls between the pair showed Berejiklian clearly wanted to avoid certain details of Maguire's business plans. In one call played by the ICAC, Berejiklian told Maguire: 'I don't need to know about that bit.' In an August 2017 call, the pair discussed potential future plans together. Berejiklian told Maguire: 'You will always be my numero uno.' Asked by the ICAC what she meant by that, Berejiklian responded: 'In my personal life I placed importance on how I felt about him.' Later, when Robertson asked Maguire if he was still in a relationship with his *hawkiss*, Maguire was sanguine: 'Oh, not after the events of this I wouldn't be, no.'

By the time Kean was back in mobile phone reception after Berejiklian gave her evidence, he had close to 100 missed calls. The first call had come from Ayres. Kean's colleagues were in complete shock and many were convinced Berejiklian would not end the day as premier. Kean was booked on a flight out of Armidale later that day but he needed to work the phones so decided to drive the 400 kilometres back to Sydney so he could talk to colleagues and keep them calm. He dumped Marshall on the side of the highway and told him he had to make his own way home.

McCormack, meanwhile, was in his Canberra office when one of his young, inexperienced media advisers interrupted an important meeting to tell his boss about the breaking news out of the ICAC. The deputy prime minister was unimpressed with his staff member spreading gossip, especially because he had also been friends with Berejiklian for many years. After he had finished editing Wagga Wagga's local newspaper, McCormack had set up his own media and publishing business. He had printed Berejiklian's electorate newsletters, in several languages, when she first entered parliament. McCormack made his views to his staff member clear: 'I said to him, I know you are young and enthusiastic but you can't just say things that you have heard on the grapevine.' The adviser pointed to the television screens that were running the news, but McCormack was not buying it. 'I kept chastising him for saying something out loud that was so obviously off the planet that it was not credible.' Finally, McCormack took a moment to read the strapline running at the bottom of the television screen. His adviser was not exaggerating and McCormack was left speechless. 'I had to pick my jaw off the ground,' he said.

McCormack kept in touch with Maguire (and Berejiklian). Despite the allegations that emerged before the ICAC, McCormack felt a degree of loyalty towards Maguire. 'You can't just turn your back on someone so if he calls me, I answer. If he texts me, I respond,'

McCormack said. But there was no denying Maguire's reputation in his home town had been destroyed, and he became an invisible figure around Wagga Wagga after Berejiklian's demise. Berejiklian's former love keeps to himself on his property, where he runs a small horse agistment business. 'I don't know anyone who has seen Daryl in town, at an event, at a pub, having a coffee, shopping and that is kind of sad. Wagga Wagga people felt let down by Maguire, especially because Gladys is a much loved figure,' said McCormack. Maguire also spends time at a property he owns in Ivanhoe, a speck of a town on the Cobb Highway in the New South Wales outback. Maguire snapped up two derelict shacks in the town of fewer than 200 people while he was still an MP, paying less than $10,000 in total, with ambitious plans to turn them into holiday rentals. It was yet another pie-in-the-sky plan from a man whose years of wheeling and dealing now threatened to derail a premier's career.

6

THE CHARM OFFENSIVE

AFTER BEREJIKLIAN'S BOMBSHELL EVIDENCE, HER POLITical career hung in the balance. The ICAC had claimed the scalp of her predecessor and mentor Barry O'Farrell after his memory lapse involving the $3000 bottle of 1959 Penfolds Grange. Like Berejiklian, O'Farrell had been called to give evidence to a corruption inquiry as nothing more than a witness, but in the process told the commission he had no recollection of receiving a bottle of vintage wine sent to him as a congratulatory gift after winning the 2011 state election.

The ICAC has an uncanny way of catching the most unsuspecting off guard and once it produced a handwritten thankyou note for the wine – signed by O'Farrell – his forgetfulness was exposed. O'Farrell resigned as premier within hours of the note surfacing rather than attempting to ride out what would have developed into a slow burn scandal for his government.

Late in the day after her ICAC appearance in October 2020, a clearly rattled Berejiklian faced the media, but unlike her former boss, it was not to resign. Her deputy and treasurer Dominic Perrottet, who had only heard the details of her romance for the first time a short time earlier, and Liberal elder and long-term ally Brad Hazzard were asked to stand by her side in a show of solidarity. Her cabinet and MPs had not been forewarned about what was coming in the ICAC inquiry, but a small group of Berejiklian's trusted advisers had been let in on her secret well ahead of time, giving them days of opportunity to prepare for the onslaught. She also warned her sisters Rita and Mary to brace for a shock and to take care of their devoted parents when the news broke.

At a press conference in the New South Wales parliament garden after her evidence wrapped up, Berejiklian put on a brave face. 'Without question I stuffed up my private life. I accept that. It's very difficult for someone in my position to have a private and personal life and I'm very upset at what has transpired. But I want to make this assurance to the people of New South Wales – I have always put the public first. I've sacrificed my life to public office and I'm proud of that.' Berejiklian's defence of her diabolical choice in a partner was that she was too trusting and was hoodwinked by a cad. She painted the whole sorry episode as a wishful schoolyard romance rather than an adult relationship, but the more she tried to explain, the more questions she raised.

Why did she not end the relationship with Maguire in 2018 when he was first named in a corruption inquiry? 'That is a very good question and can I say that initially he was very angry with me, I was extremely angry with him, I sacked him. I asked for his resignation, then I not only convinced him to leave parliament, but accosted others to help me convince him to leave parliament.' How could the public be sure that she kept her private life with Maguire separate from her public obligations? 'People may have tried to influence me, people may have tried to get around proper process, but they failed.' And the most obvious one: had she considered resigning? 'No, I haven't because I haven't done anything wrong. If I had done something wrong, I would be the first one to do that.'

Perrottet, long seen as the heir apparent to the premiership, did his best to hide his astonishment at the press conference even though he had confided in colleagues that he was slightly nervous about standing shoulder to shoulder with Berejiklian when he knew nothing more than what had transpired publicly at the ICAC. He had been visiting a building site – coincidentally with Berejiklian's good friend John Brogden, who was at the time the head of the government's property development arm – when Brogden pulled Perrottet aside and told him what was unfolding at the commission. Before he had time to digest the news, a television camera was in Perrottet's face asking for comment.

Soon after, Berejiklian phoned Perrottet to personally reassure him that she had done nothing wrong. When he faced the full press pack a short time later, Perrottet praised his boss, insisting she had the utmost integrity and honesty, and that he had never seen anyone work so hard in a job, not taking a day off despite facing bushfires, floods, drought and then the pandemic. The avuncular Hazzard was there under the pretence of delivering a health update – just one new case of COVID-19 that day – but made sure he stressed that the state would have been worse off had it not been for Berejiklian.

Meanwhile, Berejiklian pinned her hopes on garnering sympathy from the sisterhood, proclaiming she was proud to be a strong, financially independent woman. 'I just want to say to all the girls and women out there that please know that it's okay to be in public office, it's okay to make the sacrifices, but it's also okay to accept that we're far from perfect, certainly I'm far from perfect.' She was banking on the assumption that many women could empathise with having dated a dud. Her lines raised a few eyebrows from her colleagues, who wondered why someone who hated playing the gender card so vehemently would rely on it at a time like this. But Berejiklian was fighting for her political survival and needed to pull out all stops.

Former sex discrimination commissioner, Liberal MP and ABC journalist Pru Goward understood Berejiklian's predicament. 'We have all had a Daryl in our lives,' she said, referring to an all-too-familiar and unpleasant rite of passage in the lives of many women. 'Sometimes these are wolves in sheep's clothing: the sweet bloke who wouldn't hurt you but turns out to be a stalker, or a bankrupt who takes your money, or a serial philanderer with a woman in every suburb.' In Berejiklian's case, according to Goward, she dated an Arthur Daley figure – a charlatan who rarely made money on his dodgy deals but never stopped trying.

Not all Berejiklian's colleagues shared Goward's Pollyanna assessment of the situation. With O'Farrell's career implosion after his run-in with the ICAC weighing on everyone's minds, there were deep fears within Berejiklian's inner sanctum about her fate. During the days that followed her evidence, the Labor Opposition smelled blood, and moved motions of no confidence against her in both houses of parliament. Its efforts failed – although only by one vote in the upper house – and Berejiklian remained defiant. 'I provided assistance as a witness in great detail. I was forthright and direct, much to my personal detriment, but I had to do it because it is in the public interest,' she told parliament that week. 'I say to the people of New South Wales that every day that I have been in this place, since 2003, I have worked hard – my guts out – for the people. I will continue to do that.'

New South Wales Labor kept up the attack, describing Berejiklian's claims of innocence as delusional. The then Opposition leader Jodi McKay accused the premier of being a fraud: 'If you thought you knew Gladys Berejiklian, think again.' One of Berejiklian's staunchest supporters grimly warned that he was convinced that the premier was blind to the error of her ways, while another maintained that she would ride out the storm because she was loved by voters. The seasoned politician said prophetically: 'For the first time in my career we have the public and politicians on one side and the media on the other. But what we don't know is how long it stays like that and I admit it would only take one unhelpful detail to come out and everything would change.'

Extraordinarily, Labor failed to land a blow and much of the public seemed to support Berejiklian. Not long after the salacious details of her personal life were aired at the anti-corruption commission, the first bunches of flowers arrived. Then more and more. Her Parliament House office and her electorate office in Willoughby were over-flowing with floral tributes from friends, colleagues and strangers. One bunch came from a doctor on Macquarie Street, home to Australia's oldest parliament as well as Sydney's top medical specialists. The doctor had never met Berejiklian but wanted to show his support.

Later that week, she was so inundated with floral arrangements that she had to offload bunches of flowers to her staff. Her offices were also hit with a deluge of emails. Some were unforgiving, but the overwhelming bulk of the correspondence indicated the public had her back. Berejiklian received an unprecedented wave of public support that lifted her – not to mention her staff, who were worried they could soon be unemployed – during the most tumultuous week of her life.

Despite this, plenty of her colleagues remained shell-shocked, still grappling with the reality that Berejiklian may not survive the fallout. While allegations of abusing his position as an MP to clear large debts lay firmly at Maguire's feet, it was the squeaky-clean premier's judgement that was under the spotlight. How much did she really know of her boyfriend's side hustles and his use of his parliament office to peddle his questionable business interests? And why didn't she cut off all contact with him when he was forced to quit his 20-year political career under a corruption cloud? For a leader who held herself as a paragon of virtue, Berejiklian's trust in Maguire was seen by many as a serious lapse in judgement. Her best chance of survival was drawing on the significant political capital she had built through her handling of some of the toughest months her state had faced.

Her most trusted media adviser had hatched a game plan that was ready to be implemented if she needed a lifeline. The strategy was for Berejiklian to give an interview to News Corp about her heartbreak and then she would hit the commercial radio stations to tell her tale as a woman wronged by a bad boyfriend. Even the successful but controversial radio host and former *Australian Idol* judge Kyle Sandilands would get airtime with the premier. It was a high-stakes gamble and was only going to be unleashed if really needed. Despite the week from hell playing out largely in Berejiklian's favour, her team decided to proceed with the media campaign to cement her leadership and her standing with voters.

Berejiklian posed for photos chatting with *Sunday Telegraph* gossip writer Annette Sharp, whose biography on the News Corp website says she has been reporting on 'society, celebrity and sin for 25 years'. Dressed down in jeans and a blazer, a significant shift from the usual feminine floral and sharp jackets that came to define her COVID-19 11 am press conferences, the deeply private premier poured out her heart to Sharp, declaring her love for Maguire and her hopes they would one day marry. The first tell-all interview was splashed across the front page of New South Wales' biggest selling Sunday tabloid, and extended to a double-page spread inside. 'I'm never going to speak to him again. My life's changed forever,' were Berejiklian's carefully crafted words.

Described by Sharp as romantically inexperienced, Berejiklian bemoaned that having her private life laid bare before the ICAC was something that had left her 'embarrassed and humiliated' – a new low for a woman with an impeccable reputation. 'I can formally say to people I've given up on love,' she declared. She described being hauled before the ICAC and the days that followed as horrific, saying they left her feeling as though she was having an out-of-body experience. 'I'm still trying to process it. I feel like it's someone else living this. It's like I'm the main protagonist in a movie. It's like I'm the feature and the film is going to end and my life is going to go back to normal but it will never be normal again.'

Sharp later tweeted some of the words of encouragement Berejiklian received as passers-by saw her being interviewed: 'Stick it to them Glad', 'We love you Glad', 'Men are duds Glad'. The *Sunday Telegraph* also published the results of a poll it commissioned from research company YouGov which showed that women were Berejiklian's biggest backers – 70 per cent said they approved of the job she was doing as premier. Women were also more likely to believe that she had done nothing wrong when it came to Maguire and his business interests. On the question of whether Berejiklian should stay on as premier, 65 per cent of women said yes. Most men felt the same.

On the Monday after the confessional newspaper interview, Berejiklian did the rounds of Sydney's commercial radio stations, speaking first to her friend, 2GB host Ben Fordham, who had only months earlier taken over the coveted breakfast radio spot from Alan Jones. Fordham had long been a supporter of the premier; in a *Good Weekend* profile, Fordham said, 'I care about her deeply,' when asked about Berejiklian. Berejiklian has been to Fordham's birthday dinners as well as his Melbourne Cup celebrations. No one was surprised that Berejiklian chose him to help her ride out the storm. (*The Australian*'s Media Diary later revealed that Fordham was warned by 2GB management that his on-air love affair with Berejiklian had to end. He could not be mates with the premier while holding her to account.)

Fordham was straight to the point with the question everyone wanted answered: 'Why didn't you tell anybody about it? Not even your closest friends and family?'

Berejiklian: 'Because it wasn't a normal relationship, it wasn't normal, it wasn't. He wasn't my boyfriend, he wasn't anything of note. I certainly hoped it would be but it wasn't sufficiently substantial for me to say anything and because I'm not the type of person who has been in a long-term relationship, I didn't want to introduce anyone to my close network unless I knew it was the real deal and I didn't feel it was at the time.'

Fordham: 'You say he wasn't your boyfriend, but you've said you were in love with him?'

Berejiklian: 'Yeah but how many times are you in love with lots of people and it doesn't end up in something more formal, so I certainly was.'

Fordham: 'So on one hand he was not your boyfriend, on another hand you were in love with him.'

Berejiklian: 'Yeah.'

(In the months that followed, Berejiklian's media team asked that Maguire not be referred to as her lover. 'Boyfriend' was more accurate.)

Fordham ended his interview saying New South Wales would be 'mad to sacrifice the best premier we've had in so long', urging his friend to 'hang in there. Stay strong.'

Berejiklian then moved on to Kyle & Jackie O on KIIS 1065. Kyle Sandilands was another sympathetic ear. 'She went up in my opinion polls, I thought wow, look at this, this is what we want,' Sandilands declared at the start of the interview. Berejiklian admitted to Sandilands that she had shed plenty of tears and had accepted that people would pass judgement on her life choice. 'I am a private person. It has been excruciating having to talk about it. I think it's made me feel more human than I've ever felt and more vulnerable than I've ever felt,' she told him. In the usual brash Sandilands style, he said he'd always assumed Berejiklian was a lesbian. She laughed it off, not before adding there would be no problem if she was.

Not all Sydney's powerful shock jocks were on Berejiklian's side, however. Fordham's colleague at 2GB, talkback radio host Ray Hadley, was unambiguous in his views about the premier's future after her ICAC revelations. He was adamant that her actions, and staying on in the top job, did not 'pass the pub test'. Hadley was also exasperated by the Sharp interview in the *Sunday Telegraph*. 'That sounds like a 15-year-old school girl that got dudded by her boyfriend on Instagram. When someone grows a backbone in New South Wales parliament, from the Liberal side of politics, they'll stand up and say what needs to be said. Gladys, you need to have a think about your future, because I'm sorry, based on your lack of judgement in relation to this matter, you can't be premier into the future.'

A significant blunder made by the commission during the ICAC inquiry saw extremely private details of the romance between Berejiklian and Maguire inadvertently made public. The ICAC managed to accidentally upload a suppressed transcript to its website which was from a closed hearing from a private two-hour examination of Maguire focusing on the nature and extent of their relationship. The transcript was online for half an hour before anyone from the commission realised and it was swiftly pulled down.

Not surprisingly, in that small window of time journalists stumbled upon it and the transcript was downloaded more than 200 times. The commission issued an urgent suppression order that night and slapped a blanket ban on any of it being published or described in any way. The media followed the rules and did not reveal the details, but many conspiratorial Liberals were convinced that the ICAC had deliberately set out to embarrass the premier with salacious details of her private life.

Berejiklian's lawyer, Arthur Moses, lodged a complaint with the Inspector of the ICAC, Bruce McClintock SC, arguing that the security of Berejiklian's home had been compromised by the release of the transcript. McClintock's investigation put it down to human error at the hands of a junior ICAC employee, not subterfuge, but the damage had been done. The transcript landed in the hands of One Nation New South Wales leader Mark Latham.

The former federal Labor leader turned right-wing bomb thrower, who repeatedly criticised the media for not being more critical of Berejiklian, used parliamentary privilege to reveal the details of the suppressed transcript. The legal immunity that comes with parliamentary privilege has a long history of being used in the Westminster system as a way to air dirty laundry, with the most notable example being the British Profumo scandal of 1963. An affair between 19-year-old showgirl Christine Keeler and the secretary of war John Profumo was sensationally revealed to the House of Commons by a Labour MP. Keeler's simultaneous sexual liaisons with Profumo and the Soviet attaché Yevgeny Ivanov ended Profumo's political career and rocked the British government. Latham's revelations did not have the same national security implications as the Profumo scandal, but nonetheless it shook Berejiklian's camp.

Latham used the protection of parliamentary privilege in the inconspicuous upper house question time to land a punch. He pointed out that Berejiklian had made much of the fact that 'she's a very private person', despite giving recent interviews to a 'newspaper gossip writer and Kyle Sandilands' before casually adding that Maguire had a key to her lower north shore home. No one could believe Latham's audacity but his actions had the desired impact. Latham never tried to hide his disdain for Berejiklian and was adamant her undisclosed relationship was enough for her to resign. He warned he would not support any government legislation if she remained leader, a threat that he knew would cause some consternation in the hostile upper house because the government regularly had trouble getting bills passed.

His question time comments were widely reported, allowing the press gallery to run the story that they had previously been prevented from touching. Labor joined the pile-on in the lower house, with McKay asking Berejiklian why she failed to declare the romance if Maguire had a key to her house just the month earlier. Speaker Jonathan O'Dea leapt to Berejiklian's defence and tried to stop the question, citing the ICAC's suppression orders. But Berejiklian did not need O'Dea's help. She wanted to respond. 'I've read and heard things, including today, which are just factually incorrect,' she told the house, without further explanation.

The main message in Berejiklian's media offensive was that no one – not her close friends, colleagues or even her sisters – knew about her clandestine relationship that went on for at least half a decade. But Berejiklian had confided in at least one person. She had shared her closely guarded secret with her former trusted media adviser and friend Lisa Mullins. Mullins, a journalist who throughout her career has worked for ministers on both sides of politics at a state and federal level, remembers their 2015 conversation vividly. Berejiklian was giddy with excitement as she told Mullins that she was in love.

The pair met when Berejiklian was an up-and-coming MP for Willoughby and Mullins was the editor of Berejiklian's local paper, the *North Shore Times*. They struck up a friendship. Well before the New South Wales Coalition was swept to power in 2011, Mullins committed to joining Berejiklian's ministerial staff in the likely event the Liberals and Nationals were able to beat the damaged and tired Labor Party, which was ultimately reduced to a rump of just 20 lower house seats.

Mullins says Berejiklian was one of the best ministers she had worked for: hardworking, across detail and always punctual. 'Having worked for the ministers I have worked for, you do not want scandal-plagued ministers,' Mullins says. (Former New South Wales Labor minister Joe Tripodi, also a good boss according to Mullins, ended up being with a ICAC serious corrupt conduct finding against him for misusing his position as a Member of Parliament; another of her bosses, former police minister David Campbell – a 'lovely bloke' – quit cabinet after visiting a gay sex club in Sydney's eastern suburbs.) 'You want ministers who read their brief, turn up to meetings and have, at least, a vague idea of what's going on. Gladys always drove the agenda, she knew her stuff and she was a fantastic minister. She was always great to the staff, fun but professional.'

The pair stayed firm friends when Mullins moved on to pursue other jobs, including as media director for O'Farrell when he was premier. Mullins was working for the public service in 2015 when she met Berejiklian for a meal in her electorate and heard the big news. One striking element of the conversation, however, was Berejiklian's steadfast refusal to reveal the identity of her new love, stressing that it would be too much of a shock to everyone. Mullins didn't push Berejiklian on who it was, but it sent her mind racing. Her best guess was that it was Nick Greiner. Greiner, at the time, was chair of Infrastructure NSW and he had a long history of sparring with Berejiklian as transport minister as she tried to deliver her pet light rail project. Mullins assumed their fractured relationship was a ruse to hide an affair. After all, Greiner would be the right calibre for Berejiklian.

Mullins was wrong about Greiner, but it didn't matter who Berejiklian's man was. Mullins was thrilled to see her friend 'glowing in love'; it was the first time the veteran media spinner had heard Berejiklian speak of any romantic interest. Berejiklian told Mullins of her desire to have a baby with her new partner, but that she was worried about the political implications and the media fallout. At the time, Berejiklian was in her 40s and Mullins did not want her to wait too long. They discussed a media strategy to deal with Berejiklian's hopeful pregnancy, and Mullins promised to write a press release if the time came to make an announcement. Over the years, Mullins did not probe Berejiklian on the relationship and Berejiklian did not offer any more details, but Mullins was gobsmacked when the identity of her friend's boyfriend was revealed five years later.

The last time Mullins was in contact with Berejiklian was to wish her a happy 50th birthday in September 2020. The next month, Berejiklian's shock evidence about her relationship with Maguire was revealed publicly to the ICAC and Mullins was left horrified by the lengths Berejiklian went to save her political career. Mullins was lost for words and did not contact Berejiklian again because she had no idea what to say.

Mullins lamented: 'What really aggravated me about this whole thing was Glad always wanted to get promoted on merit, was against quotas and made much of the fact that she got where she was on her own, not by an artificial means. And yet when push came to shove, she really played the "poor, poor pitiful me, I got dudded by a bad boyfriend" line.

'From a female perspective, I just found that quite repugnant. I understand, politically, it was probably a smart thing to do but I did find it galling. If that was me, I couldn't have done that because she completely turned her back on all her previously articulated principles.'

Berejiklian's gamble paid off. Her tell-all interviews saw her not only survive but thrive, seemingly untouched by the scandal. In the weeks that followed, Berejiklian resumed normal service and the frenzy around her failed romance was overtaken by COVID-19 recovery as the state slowly returned to life-before-pandemic. Berejiklian was also at pains to tell her ministers, or at least those she trusted and respected the most, that her dalliance with Maguire was her first and only romance. She privately spoke to them about the relationship, worried that she would be judged by them for her poor choice in men. Despite feeling awkward about their boss discussing an intimate relationship, they sensed a raw vulnerability as well as a deep-seated insecurity and shame. They did their best to assure her that they had her back. Perhaps that buoyed her, or maybe it was the overwhelming response she received from the public and friendly shock jocks that made the difference.

Whatever it was, Berejiklian wasted no time in insisting that a line should be drawn under the saga when the media tried to push her on the relationship. At a fiery press conference just two days after her ICAC appearance, a visibly angry Berejiklian made it clear that she would not keep going over old ground. 'I say to the people of this great state, you elected me, you deserve me to be focused on you. You deserve for me to be focused on the issues that matter to you. And that is exactly what I will do. I know the people of this state know I have done nothing wrong. I never have and I never will. I appreciate the questions you will need to ask, and I've answered them in full detail over the course of a number of days. But you also have to respect my position as premier. Let me do my job,' she said.

Berejiklian's very targeted public relations campaign was seen by many as a media masterstroke, with a senior Labor adviser to Victorian Premier Daniel Andrews messaging Berejiklian's media director Sean Berry to congratulate him on what he saw as a brilliant strategy. However, not everyone in Berejiklian's camp was convinced it would prove to be a wise move long term. The concern was that Berejiklian had downplayed the seriousness of the relationship when she was before the ICAC, only to walk out and paint a very different picture to save her political career.

This was not lost on the anti-corruption commission. During the ICAC's later probe into Berejiklian, her barrister Sophie Callan SC wanted parts of the evidence about the romance with Maguire to be heard in private, to spare the former premier from any humiliation. The commissioner Ruth McColl could not be convinced that Berejiklian's privacy needed to be protected. Counsel assisting Scott Robertson tabled 40 pages of newspaper clippings and radio interviews from Berejiklian's post-ICAC media blitz. McColl later revealed in a written ruling that: 'It is not irrelevant in my view to note that soon after Ms Berejiklian gave evidence in the 2020 public inquiry, she made public statements concerning the nature and extent of her relationship with Mr Maguire, described as a "radio blitz" by one publication.' She pointed out that Berejiklian used radio interviews to talk about how she 'loved Maguire and hoped he could be her boyfriend' and also 'hoped the relationship could lead to marriage'.

McColl's thoughts on the matter were clear. 'In the light of Ms Berejiklian's preparedness in 2020 to engage in public disclosures of her private relationship, it is difficult to accept Ms Callan's submission, that further public disclosures will entail a risk of undue prejudice in the sense of leading to intense and irremediable publicity, public scrutiny, humiliation and irreparable harm.' Berejiklian's charm offensive had bought more time, but had not endeared her to those running the investigation.

7

THE QUEEN BEE

When then foreign minister Julie Bishop strode out to the Senate courtyard of Parliament House on a wintery Canberra morning in late August 2018, her red satin pumps with bejewelled heels stood out among a sea of blue suits and RM Williams boots. After one of the most tumultuous periods in federal politics, which saw Malcolm Turnbull's prime ministership spectacularly implode after he could not stare down opposition from conservative dissidents over a national energy guarantee, the most senior Liberal woman on the federal frontbench was quitting. Not politics (at that stage), but Bishop was announcing her decision not to serve in Scott Morrison's revamped cabinet. She would sit out the remainder of her long political career on the backbench as the MP for Curtin.

Bishop described those now famous shoes as 'comfortable work boots', although no one really bought that (RM Williams, on the other hand, are just that). Given her penchant for using the red stiletto emoji in text messages – a 'statement of women's empowerment', according to Bishop – the shoes were clearly designed to send a message. 'When in doubt wear red,' Bishop later told the *Sydney Morning Herald*. Bishop's ruby Dorothy slippers quickly came to symbolise the Liberals' women problem. Veteran political commentator Tony Wright dubbed what came next the Red Shoe Resistance.

It began with Bishop, but several Liberals in the sisterhood soon joined the movement. Less than a month after Morrison took over the leadership, Victorian backbencher Julia Banks – who was so disgusted by bullying during the party's internal civil war that she ultimately quit politics – wore a red power suit and fire-engine red heels to question time. Then minister for women Kelly O'Dwyer (who also chose not to stick around in politics) wore a claret-coloured blazer. Backbenchers Nicolle Flint and Ann Sudmalis were also in red. Wright wrote of that day: 'There seemed rather more than a wry hint of *The Handmaid's Tale* – the TV series, based on Margaret Atwood's book, in which totalitarian (male) leaders subjugate women, preventing them from working, owning property, handling money, or reading. Oh, yes, and handmaids wear red.' When Bishop later that year donated her iconic once-worn heels to the Museum of Australian Democracy, author and host of the ABC's *The Drum*, Julia Baird, described the sparkly pumps as 'symbols of defiance, spunk and covert rebellion'.

The very day after the Red Shoe Resistance marched into federal question time, Berejiklian arrived at New South Wales parliament wearing striking red heels. There were no sparkles, but they were stylish and a shift from her usual choice of more sensible footwear. Berejiklian's most senior staff member, Sarah Cruickshank, quickly killed off the idea that her boss had deliberately worn red pumps in solidarity with her Canberra sisters. When asked about Berejiklian's shoes on that day, of all days, Cruickshank responded gruffly that surely it was no longer appropriate to discuss what a female leader was wearing. Berejiklian loved to talk about clothes and was always open about her interest in fashion, often complimenting women on their outfits. Discussing her shoes would not have been offensive to her. Nevertheless, the memo had not reached Berejiklian's office, or at least the coverage of the Red Shoe Resistance had totally passed them by. Berejiklian's shoe choice was a sartorial coincidence, not a political statement.

Berejiklian, once she was premier, steered clear of bold public declarations. She saw her role as sticking to 'core business', although not before pointing out on election night 2019 that her victory showed that 'someone with a long surname – and a woman – can be the premier of New South Wales'. Several years later, she was asked why she shied away from speaking about gender issues. Her answer was simple: 'It's not about me.' Earlier in her political career, however, Berejiklian was more prepared to weigh in, especially when it came to female representation in public life. In 2015, not long after she became the first female treasurer of New South Wales, Berejiklian was the guest speaker at a Women in Banking and Finance event in Sydney. Even then, she was one of the most powerful women in Australia. She spoke about how too often she was the only woman in the room at a boardroom lunch. In a bid to change the gender makeup of such lunches, her office made it a practice to insist – as a condition of her acceptance – on having other women attend to help encourage diversity and networking opportunities for them. 'I found even when I did that, for whatever reason, the women are still not there. And I can't work out whether it is because people are too busy to rustle them up, or the women don't want to come.'

Berejiklian was brutally honest in her speech at the women in banking event, revealing not only her desire to get more women into politics, but also exposing her anxiety around playing the gender card. 'A few years ago, I probably would not have spoken at a forum such as this for fear of being stereotyped or not being judged for my achievements, but rather being judged in the context of my gender. Fortunately, I have seen the error of my ways,' she said. 'Whilst it is logical to argue that we need more women in parliament because we make up half the population and it's the right thing to do – this is not the most compelling argument.' She said it was vital to have more women in parliament because the different approaches to decision-making 'make for stronger government and better outcomes for our state and national wellbeing'. Berejiklian's message was clear. 'Gender balance is a necessity, not a nice to have, and this sense of urgency needs to drive our approach to collectively fixing the problem of female under-representation.'

Berejiklian acknowledged that the biggest hurdle for women was not surviving politics, but simply getting a start in the boys' club. 'The odds of getting preselected are well and truly stacked against women. The way to overcome this is for each major political party, including my own, to set targets for the number of women preselected in winnable seats – both upper and lower houses – at every election. These deliberate targets should be kept in place until at least 50 per cent of our elected representatives are female.'

By the time Berejiklian left New South Wales politics in 2021, after leading the state party for almost five years, no gains had been made. Two Liberal women were in cabinet and of the 44 Liberal MPs only 13 were female. When defending the Coalition government's record on appointing senior women, Berejiklian's default was to highlight that she was the state's first elected female premier, and the first female transport minister and treasurer (one woman, three positions), and that Gabrielle Upton was New South Wales' first female attorney-general in 2015. However, the party did not attract women into parliament. In March 2021, as women raged over revelations of gender discrimination that had emerged in the country's halls of power, Berejiklian said she was open-minded about quotas for the Liberal Party. 'I think targets have failed us. We haven't succeeded in getting specific targets,' she conceded. 'We do need to have that conversation, but it doesn't begin and end with quotas.'

When Berejiklian had a cabinet vacancy that would have allowed her to promote a woman and boost the number of Liberal women with a ministry to three (including herself), she instead pushed for her upper house colleague Natasha Maclaren-Jones to be appointed president of the New South Wales Legislative Council. It is considered a plum role, which comes with a $300,000 salary, extra staff and an impressive office that once hosted Queen Elizabeth. However, the role is decided by a vote of the house, not by appointment, and Berejiklian's intervention backfired. The upper house voted for a man. Similarly, Berejiklian's eventual replacement in her blue-ribbon Liberal seat of Willoughby was also a man, despite her party acknowledging that it needed to stop running women in non-winnable seats, while men were handed safe seats. Berejiklian had tried her best to back a woman to succeed her, but preselectors chose the conservative Tim James, who came very close to losing Willoughby for the Liberals in a by-election after she resigned, despite inheriting a huge margin from Berejiklian.

In 2021, the pandemic in New South Wales remained Berejiklian's overriding focus, but it was a brave young woman who generated and dominated debate in Canberra and beyond. Grace Tame was a sexual assault survivor whose case led to the overturning of a Tasmanian law gagging her from speaking about her assault. She was named 2021 Australian of the Year. Tame had won a Supreme Court exemption in 2019 which allowed her to talk about how, as a 15-year-old, she was repeatedly sexually abused by her 58-year-old maths teacher. As Tame's public profile increased, she helped spark a cultural reckoning in Canberra. Women were starting to speak out about the toxicity of Parliament House as a workplace, and the ramifications for other jurisdictions, including New South Wales, made leaders such as Berejiklian uneasy. In a move that surprised her ministerial colleagues, Berejiklian made references in cabinet to the dangers of 'unconscious bias' around gender. It was puzzling for her colleagues, because Berejiklian had always steered away from such issues. They wondered whether she was being sincere with her concerns, or whether she simply felt obligated, albeit awkwardly, to acknowledge the debate that was gathering pace across the country.

On the back of Tame's award, Melbourne academic Janine Hendry pondered on Twitter how many 'extremely disgruntled' women it would take to link arms around Parliament House and stand in protest against discrimination and alleged sexual abuse in the nation's capital. Apparently, the answer was 3770 women, according to one of Hendry's mathematically minded Twitter followers. 'Ok, thanks, now to find 4000 angry women and their supporters,' Hendry responded. That was not hard. Within two weeks, more than 40 protest marches – known collectively as Women's March 4 Justice – were planned across the country to coincide with federal parliament resuming on 15 March. Berejiklian did not take part. Her office was unimpressed when the *Sydney Morning Herald* reported that the premier would not be at the Sydney march (the paper also noted that then Labor leader Jodi McKay was also not planning to attend, although she had a late change of heart).

When Hendry was asked for her thoughts on Berejiklian and McKay skipping the Sydney event, she did not sugarcoat her thoughts: 'In light of what's happening, not only in parliament but other major institutions, when our very own representatives don't want to hear our voice, what does that say about how they really think about women?

It's saying we don't matter, and they don't want to hear our voices and that's not okay.' Berejiklian's office was furious that Hendry was given a forum to criticise the premier in such a public way. Queensland premier Annastacia Palaszczuk joined one of the marches in her state, but Berejiklian said she counted herself among the thousands of women who supported the cause but could not get to a march because of work or family commitments.

New South Wales Minister for Women and Nationals MP Bronnie Taylor later offered a half-hearted defence of Berejiklian: 'A march is not Gladys' thing, she is not one to use a public display to voice her opinions.' However, another senior Coalition woman was less forgiving. 'Is Gladys supportive of women? No. Does she help galvanise women? No. You only have to look at her cabinet to see she doesn't promote women.' Indeed, her closest male colleagues often commented that she felt more comfortable in their company. One said: 'She definitely looks up to powerful men.' Five MPs from the Coalition took part in the march, including John Barilaro, Attorney-General Mark Speakman and Matt Kean, as well as vocal feminists Liberal MP Felicity Wilson and Taylor. Barilaro said he was not there to make a statement, but 'to watch, listen and engage'.

Two days after the march, Berejiklian revealed in question time that she had quietly appointed Pru Goward, the former sex discrimination commissioner and one-time Liberal minister, to formally review the practice for ministerial staff making complaints about bullying, harassment or sexual assault. She said she approached Goward because she was so moved by hearing horror stories of political workplace culture. 'I chose at the time not to do this publicly because I wanted to make sure that all processes we have in place are as robust and as precise and as fair and transparent as they need to be. I want the report to come to me directly,' Berejiklian told the parliament. Goward was asked to look into how staff go about making a complaint about bullying, harassment or sexual misconduct in the workplace.

Berejiklian's decision was not well received across the chamber. Greens MP Jenny Leong said it was inappropriate that a former Liberal minister be tasked with carrying out such a review. Labor's whip Anna Watson demanded to know why she had not been asked to be involved, given her role in her party. 'I have women coming into my office from all over this parliament complaining about bullying and harassment,' she said. However, the review was only looking into Berejiklian's own.

When Goward handed down her report just a month later, she found that political ambition, loyalty to ministers and the tenuous nature of their employment was leaving ministerial staff reluctant to report misconduct. Berejiklian described the report as 'brutal'. In her strongly worded response, Goward said the 'protections and processes available to ministerial staff are unclear, ineffective and inadequate'. Goward also found that the ability to obtain government information through freedom of information or orders from the upper house could be barriers for complaints, with fears that the complainants' concerns would become public knowledge. Goward's review, however, only focused on government ministers and their staff. This prompted parliament's presiding officers to appoint another former sex discrimination commissioner, Elizabeth Broderick, to carry out a wide-ranging investigation into Australia's oldest parliament, examining complaints handling and support systems for employees from MPs to staffers, cleaners, press gallery reporters and security and hospitality workers. That report was due in mid 2022.

Berejiklian may have steered clear of making overt statements on gender, but she had previously played a key role in one of the most significant women's rights issues to be considered by the New South Wales parliament. In 2019, she was a driving force in the decriminalisation of abortion in the state. Incredibly, her state was the last in the country where termination was still considered a crime. The parliament had dealt with what was seen as the precursor to abortion reform in the final months of the previous parliamentary term. The progressive upper house Nationals MP Trevor Khan, who later left politics for a judicial appointment as a magistrate, was one of the co-sponsors of a 2018 bill which meant protesters could face jail time if they harassed people outside abortion clinics and hospitals that provided terminations. Safe access zones, which provide a buffer around abortion clinics that protesters cannot access, had already been legislated in Victoria, Tasmania, the Australian Capital Territory and the Northern Territory. Berejiklian, who granted her Liberal MPs a conscience vote on the issue, voted in favour of the bill.

The very night the safe zones legislation passed the New South Wales lower house in 2018, Khan and his Labor upper house colleague Penny Sharpe started planning their next campaign. Khan said: 'It was obvious to us both that the numbers were there in each house to pass an abortion reform bill. We decided that abortion reform would be the first issue we would tackle in the next parliament, and that a bill should be introduced as soon as possible in the new parliamentary term.' Khan got to work. He could not ask the Office of Parliamentary Counsel to draft a bill without the approval of the premier's office, which Khan did not want to seek because it would put Berejiklian in a difficult position. Independent Sydney MP Alex Greenwich, however, did not face the same constraints. Khan also knew there was the possibility that the looming 2019 state election, which was less than a year away, could see the Coalition in minority government, leaving Greenwich perfectly placed to advance abortion reform from a position of strength. The stars were aligning. Safe access zones had already caused great angst within the Liberals, so Khan knew Greenwich was the person to take the lead.

Berejiklian's strategy on abortion was to stay out of the heat of battle and generate an impression that the reform – long sought by women's groups and most health professionals – was an inevitability and out of her hands. To an extent this was correct. The bill was introduced by Greenwich, who had already started work on his legislation, with Khan's guidance, before the 2019 election. By the time it was finally introduced to the parliament, Berejiklian had returned the Coalition to government and become the first elected female premier. There were 15 MPs co-sponsoring the abortion decriminalisation bill, which at that time was the largest number for any bill in the parliament's history. Health Minister Brad Hazzard was one of the sponsors. Berejiklian stayed in the wings while Hazzard and Andrew Constance – who was then also manager of government business – took on the task of ushering the bill through with Greenwich.

The abortion debate was the most politically bruising period in Berejiklian's premiership. Her detractors waited for her to fly to Europe on a trade mission in August before starting to cause trouble. Berejiklian and her jobs minister Stuart Ayres went to spruik Sydney's second airport – Western Sydney Airport – hoping to convince major

European organisations such as defence company BAE Systems to deliver a new space and research centre at the airport precinct. As she travelled to London to talk about the ramifications for the state post-Brexit, and then on to Germany, her colleagues back in New South Wales were in open warfare. Berejiklian would hold press conferences with German company executives by her side, but all the Australian journalists' questions were focused on the abortion debate tearing apart the Liberals back in Sydney. It would have been a puzzling spectacle for the German executives to witness a press pack only interested in abortion reform, not least because abortion is still a crime in Germany. The debate became so venomous within her party that Berejiklian faced threats of a move on her leadership – albeit from three fringe Liberal MPs from the religious right – as well as defections from members who were so incensed by the issue being allowed to surface that they considered moving to the crossbench. At times, it looked like abortion reform could end her premiership.

Greenwich said despite the extreme pressure she came under, Berejiklian remained highly supportive of what he and his backers were trying to achieve and was a constant source of encouragement. 'She stayed very focused, she wasn't going to play their games or be accused of some secret deal with me,' Greenwich said. 'There was no deal, she just believed that it was time for reform.' The MP was disgusted by the treatment Berejiklian received from her own party. 'The hard right of the Liberal Party used the abortion debate to try to destabilise the first popularly elected female premier in New South Wales,' Greenwich said. Despite the internal party conflict that was unleashed on her, Berejiklian was undeterred. She continued to offer Greenwich advice and counsel. When the legislation to bring New South Wales in line with the rest of the county came to a vote, Berejiklian sat at the back of the chamber. Some criticised her for that stance, but she knew what she was doing. Greenwich said her decision to not speak to the bill in the parliament was not about hiding from the issue. Rather, she did not want to have any influence over her colleagues in an issue so personal. The bill passed the lower house, 59 votes to 31, but the Liberal ranks were bitterly split: 14 for and 19 against. Many within the right wing of the party never forgave Berejiklian for allowing the debate to go ahead.

Abortion reform nearly ended Berejiklian's leadership but she went on to survive an even bigger onslaught that many men may not have. Of course, plenty of men do survive scandal. Deputy Prime Minister Barnaby Joyce resurrected his political career after spending more than two years on the backbench after resigning amid sexual harassment allegations made by businesswoman and former Western Australian Rural Woman of the Year Catherine Marriott. (Joyce vehemently denied the allegations, calling them 'spurious and defamatory'. He has never been charged with any crime relating to the allegations, and an investigation by the National Party took the matter no further.) Joyce's resignation followed two weeks of intense media pressure after the *Daily Telegraph* revealed the married father of four had had an affair with former staffer Vikki Campion and she was pregnant with their 'love child'. But after biding his time and waiting for his successor Michael McCormack to take a hit in the opinion polls, Joyce made his move in June 2021 and defeated McCormack in a leadership spill. Barnaby was back and all was forgiven, it seemed.

Meanwhile, when former attorney-general Christian Porter called time on his ministerial and, ultimately, political career, it was not because of accusations of improper conduct levelled against him (which he has vehemently denied and in relation to which no charges have ever been brought). Despite weeks of pressure around the allegations, the issue that finally forced Porter to quit politics was the fallout from his confirmation that he used a blind trust to bankroll some of his legal fees in his defamation action against the ABC and its reporter Louise Milligan.

Julia Baird's revised and republished *Media Tarts*, a book about how the Australian media portrays female politicians, was released in July 2021 – after Berejiklian's first appearance at the anti-corruption commission but before the final implosion of her career. Writing in the *Sydney Morning Herald*, Baird lamented that her book was 'still alarmingly relevant, in the middle of a maelstrom of female discontent' almost 20 years after she wrote the original. Baird singled out Berejiklian as someone who may have actually been saved by the media covering details of her private life. 'The one politician, in my view, who has actually benefited from being single and female is the currently beleaguered NSW Premier Gladys Berejiklian. The fact that she survived the revelations at ICAC about her relationship with disgraced MP Daryl Maguire was astounding,' Baird wrote. 'People related to her, felt sorry for her and, as she told her story to mainstream media outlets – Kyle & Jackie O at KIIS 1065, Mamamia, Ben Fordham at 2GB – the sympathy flowed for a woman who had long been unpartnered and made a surprising choice to secretly date a compromised loser. Interviewers hummed and haa-ed, expressed sorry for the embarrassment of her whole situation and ICAC, somehow, faded away.'

Throughout her career, Berejiklian liked to boast that she was married to her job. She saw it as a point of pride. She devoted her life to her career, seemingly giving up on meaningful relationships and having children in order to rise to the top. But when her romance with an undesirable man was so stunningly revealed, the public did not turn on her. Instead, as Baird pointed out, support for her only grew. Her approval ratings were sky high. It prompted some of her colleagues to wonder whether the outcome would have been the same if roles were reversed. Had Berejiklian been a male premier who committed the sin of loving the wrong woman, would he have survived?

Michelle Ryan – a professor of social and organisational psychology and the inaugural director of the Global Institute for Women's Leadership at the Australian National University, founded and chaired by former prime minister Julia Gillard – described Berejiklian as 'Tefloncoated'. This seemingly explained how she managed to weather the storm unleashed after the Maguire revelations. 'Gladys is very steady, very contained. What people often don't like in female leaders is that they are seen as emotional and unpredictable and she is just the complete opposite to that, she is so steadfast. She is unflappable.' Ryan said Berejiklian was able to be a female leader without being seen as a 'mother figure or a wife figure'. 'If anything, she was Aunty Gladys,' Ryan said.

Like many female leaders, there was an expectation for Berejiklian to champion women. Ryan said female politicians who climb to the top – whether it be former US presidential candidate Hillary Clinton, Gillard or Berejiklian – were often expected to pull women up with them. If they didn't, they risked being labelled Queen Bees. Queen Bee syndrome was coined in a 1973 US study by three psychologists at the University of Michigan. The study suggested women in senior positions were not only unsupportive of other women but actively worked to keep their female rivals out. Ryan said women leaders were often left in an impossible position regardless of what they did. 'Women who are on the way up might talk about gender but once they reach the top, throw that away. They do that because they feel they have no choice.'

Ryan concedes it is a conundrum. Female leaders who become overly focused on gender face being criticised for ignoring half the population in a quest to only represent women. Yet female leaders who don't speak about gender can come up against claims of turning their back on the sisterhood. 'If a woman talks too much about gender she will be accused of playing the woman card but men don't get accused of playing the man card. They are just playing cards,' she said. Ryan said Clinton was often accused of overstating the issue of gender during her second tilt for the White House. During the first Democratic debate in mid-October 2015, Clinton gave an opening statement that showed she intended to make gender a pillar of her campaign strategy: 'Yes, finally fathers will be able to say to their daughters, you too can grow up to be president.' Of course, male presidential candidates faced no such criticism.

In March 2021, when Berejiklian was being pressed on quotas and female representation, she made it abundantly clear that she did not want to be remembered for playing the gender card. 'I hope in history, people don't refer to me as a female premier. I hope they just refer to me as a premier,' she said.

8

THE WOMAN WHO SAVED AUSTRALIA

WHEN NEW SOUTH WALES WOKE TO A NEW DAWN ON 1 January 2020, there was little to celebrate. There was none of the usual optimism that comes with the clock hitting midnight as Sydney partied under the sparkle of multimillion-dollar firework displays. The world-famous pyrotechnics went ahead, spared at the last minute despite calls for them to be cancelled as vast swathes of the state burned. The bushfires had started in the winter of 2019 but had reached a frightening ferocity by October. Deputy Premier John Barilaro, who was holidaying in the UK over Christmas and New Year, wanted Sydney's fireworks cancelled. From wintery London, Barilaro weighed in, tweeting: 'The risk is too high and we must respect our exhausted RFS volunteers. If regional areas have had fireworks banned, then let's not have two classes of citizens. We're all in this crisis together.' His intervention had no impact. There was little appetite for partying but the Rural Fire Service gave the tick for Sydney's show to go on.

Meanwhile, holidaymakers in the southern coastal areas of New South Wales were stranded, some making dangerous and desperate escapes out of sleepy beach towns near the Victorian border. Others had been evacuated on New Year's Eve, when fire conditions were considered catastrophic. There were more than 660 separate fire incidents that day in New South Wales, 565 of them new outbreaks. Residents of the New South Wales South Coast had been in a state of anxiety since fires started in the Currowan state forest weeks earlier. From a single lightning strike, the spark quickly turned into a deadly giant that destroyed hundreds of homes and burned through 500,000 hectares. On New Year's Eve, that fire claimed the lives of three people: two who stayed to defend their homes and another who was overrun by fire in his car.

Early on New Year's Day, Berejiklian and the Rural Fire Service Commissioner Shane Fitzsimmons made the potentially life-threatening decision to fly to the South Coast to witness the devastation firsthand. On a Rural Fire Service charter flight, they managed to land at Moruya Airport, which was shrouded in smoke.

They flew knowing there was a chance it could be too risky to land. Berejiklian and Fitzsimmons were met by the local Bega MP and transport minister Andrew Constance. Constance had spent New Year's Eve trying to save his home in nearby Malua Bay and was shaken to the core. 'Glad and Shane risked their lives that day,' Constance later said. Berejiklian and Fitzsimmons toured some of the towns ravaged by the firestorm less than 24 hours earlier. An orange hue hung ominously over the usually idyllic beach holiday area. At one stage, the vehicle that the premier and commissioner were travelling in drove down a road lined with blackened trees. They turned around and headed back along the same street only minutes later. In that short time, a huge tree had fallen across their path. That they had been spared from what could have been a horrific outcome was not lost on anyone in their group. The panic was palpable but Berejiklian remained calm and composed.

Rosedale, a beachside hamlet 18 kilometres south of Batemans Bay, was one of the hardest hit towns in that area of the South Coast. Every street lost at least one home; 84 were razed in total. A group of five families who had been holidaying together for decades had to be evacuated from the township on New Year's Eve as the fire raged around them. A local family in nearby Tomakin took them in for the night – all 27 people, as well as their two rabbits and four dogs. When it was safe the next morning, the five families returned to Rosedale to collect their belongings, which they had abandoned as they fled the inferno.

Berejiklian and Fitzsimmons dropped into Rosedale on New Year's Day. The premier hugged and listened to the traumatised family members, who were aged between four and 80. With all electricity and telecommunications down, some were worried that their relatives would be desperate to hear from them. Berejiklian took down phone numbers, and promised to touch base with their loved ones. Soon after, once her ministerial car left Rosedale and reached high enough ground to receive a mobile signal, Berejiklian asked her driver to pull over so she could personally call those on her list, to reassure them that their friends and family were safe.

Fitzsimmons, who had been appointed by short-term Labor premier Nathan Rees as commissioner a decade earlier, had been planning his retirement from the Rural Fire Service. That changed once he saw what the state was facing that summer. He decided he had one more fire season in him and devoted his final months in the role to overseeing the worst bushfires in the state's history. Fitzsimmons would also spend every waking moment with Berejiklian for four months. That would test the closest of friendships, but he said he only ever had one disagreement with her during the fire crisis. In the very early days of what would become the Black Summer fires, which followed an unprecedented 1000 blazes each month during winter, he urged the premier to join him at the Rural Fire Service press conferences. Berejiklian point-blank refused, believing media briefings should be focused on the operational side of bushfires, not politicians. Fitzsimmons persisted. He felt she would add gravitas to the briefings and the public – or citizens, as was her preferred term – needed to hear from their leader. It was October and the fires had already turned deadly, with two elderly people killed in their isolated farmhouse in northern New South Wales.

Berejiklian finally relented and joined Fitzsimmons at a press conference. The pair stood shoulder to shoulder every day from that moment on to face the media, answer questions and, at times, deliver tragic news. Their daily press conferences continued until February. 'I have no doubt that it set her up for the tempo of the pandemic,' Fitzsimmons said. 'She saw the importance of not speaking about the operational side of things which is a good message for other politicians. Instead, she offered kindness and support and spoke about the people she met on the ground.'

Neither Berejiklian nor Fitzsimmons took a single day off during the whole crisis. The state's emergency services minister David Elliott, however, flew to London just after Christmas. Berejiklian had approved his leave, wanting him to have some family time after the deaths of his father and father-in-law. It was a quick trip; Fitzsimmons called Elliott as soon as he landed, and told him he was needed back in Sydney. Elliott turned around at Heathrow airport and flew home to face the ongoing emergency. Berejiklian felt so guilty about Elliott cutting his holiday short she bought him a six pack of beer to apologise.

Fitzsimmons, who has worked under many emergency services ministers as well as several premiers, views Berejiklian in a different light to other political leaders. 'She taught me to be truthful, be respectful and to leave egos at the door. She always told me to focus on the people and ignore all the noise,' he said, in a veiled reference to the media, which Berejiklian did not trust. Fitzsimmons recalls visiting the Horsley Park Rural Fire Service brigade in western Sydney with Berejiklian just after the deaths of two of their firefighters, Andrew O'Dwyer and Geoffrey Keaton. The men, both in their 30s, were Rural Fire Service volunteers who were killed when their truck rolled off the road after hitting a fallen tree. Berejiklian sat with the mourning volunteers and listened. 'She had a human touch and the ability to empathise. She was never intrusive and would just pause and listen. People saw a sincerity in her, there was no arrogance or ego about her,' Fitzsimmons said.

Fitzsimmons and Berejiklian did at least 50 field trips together to fire-damaged areas across the state during the months of the bushfire crisis, sometimes with media in tow but often not. She preferred it that way. Fitzsimmons said: 'There was never a hostile reception to her, not once.'

The prime minister, on the other hand, had a very different experience. Scott Morrison was already on shaky ground after his controversial decision to take his wife Jenny and their two daughters on a holiday to Hawaii as the nation began to burn. The whole saga was made worse when Morrison's office tried to deflect media questions, insisting the prime minister's holiday plans were 'not a story'. Speaking to 2GB from Hawaii, the prime minister delivered the infamous line: 'I don't hold a hose, mate, and I don't sit in a control room.' He issued a statement saying he 'regretted any offence caused' by his decision to take his holiday and said he would return home early, although it seemed that was on an already-booked flight.

It was not surprising, then, that Morrison did not get a rousing reception when he visited the Bega Valley township of Cobargo. In fact, it could not have been worse for the prime minister. New South Wales government officials warned Morrison's office against visiting the small timber town but his advisers persisted. Three people had died and others lost homes, businesses and livestock when the fire hit Cobargo. The prime minister, his entourage and television cameras were not warmly received.

Morrison was forced to abandon a meet and greet in the town's main street when he was confronted by angry residents. 'How are you?' Morrison asked, as he approached one woman who had her hands firmly by her side. He reached out, took her hand and started shaking it. The woman responded: 'I'm only shaking your hand if you give more funding to our RFS.' To make matters worse, footage captured by TV cameras showed Morrison approaching a firefighter, again offering his hand. 'I don't really want to shake your hand,' the firefighter said. Morrison awkwardly picked up the man's hand, before getting the message and walking off.

Berejiklian and Morrison's ways of handling the fire disaster were polar opposites. Fitzsimmons lost track of the number of evacuation centres he visited with Berejiklian, but she would never accept even a bottle of water, despite the stifling conditions. She wanted to keep all supplies for those who needed them. But she would shout lunch. Fitzsimmons says they stopped for fish and chips one day (Berejiklian had a salad) but debit cards could not be used because the power was down in the area. 'She said, "Of course I have cash, I am ethnic." And she paid for us all.' When Fitzsimmons finally managed to carry out his retirement plans, Berejiklian appointed him to a newly created agency, making him the commissioner of Resilience NSW, a body designed to help rebuild after disasters. She did not want to lose her trusted right-hand man altogether.

The veil of smoke from the Black Summer bushfires – which killed 26 people, destroyed 2448 homes and burnt 5.5 million hectares of land – had barely lifted when Berejiklian found herself confronting a second crisis that would engulf New South Wales. Reports out of Wuhan, ground zero for COVID-19, had been worrying Australian health experts from the very early days of 2020. Epidemiologists were growing increasingly concerned as they watched cases multiply overseas by the day. Berejiklian had barely slept over the summer months as bushfires raged. But what was unleashed on her and the people of New South Wales would ensure Berejiklian faced two sleepless years. By the end of January, the inevitable occurred and the virus slipped the borders and arrived in New South Wales.

It did not take long for the first COVID-19 crisis to hit New South Wales. After an 11-day voyage, the *Ruby Princess* cruise ship returned to Sydney just before dawn on 19 March, cutting short its final New Zealand leg because Prime Minister Jacinda Ardern had announced a travel ban. That morning the ship's 2647 passengers were allowed to disembark at Sydney's Circular Quay, wander around the harbour and travel home in taxis and rideshares. Despite obvious cases of respiratory illnesses on board, passengers were shepherded off the *Ruby Princess* in record time.

Seasoned traveller William Wright, a retired stockbroker, later gave a statement to investigators: 'I am a regular traveller overseas by flights and cruises. I have never experienced something so fast.' Just days after the ship docked, Health Minister Brad Hazzard was already acknowledging that, with the benefit of hindsight, passengers should not have been allowed to disembark until the results of COVID-19 tests were known. 'If I had my opportunity to have my two bobs' worth, with the benefit of what we now know about those people I'd have said yeah, maybe we should hold them on the ship,' Hazzard said.

There were also onboard failings. One passenger, Paul Reid, revealed a male doctor on board the cruise ship took a swab from his nose and throat, dipped it 'in a mixture', then told him: 'You don't have corona, you have the common cold.' Reid later tested positive for COVID-19. Josephine Roope, whose friend Lesley Bacon died of COVID-19 after their ill-fated voyage, reported that the ship's medical staff told her three times that her friend only had the flu, even though Bacon had tested negative for influenza. The *Ruby Princess* turned out to be the single largest superspreader event in Australia, at one point responsible for more than 10 per cent of the country's cases.

The *Ruby Princess* name became synonymous with failings within the New South Wales health department. In the weeks that followed, 663 Australian passengers and 191 crew tested positive to COVID-19 and

28 people died. The government and Hazzard were heavily criticised and NSW Labor called for the health minister's resignation as well as a probe into the debacle. In April, Berejiklian announced a special commission of inquiry into the *Ruby Princess* to be led by the government's go-to barrister, Bret Walker SC. After 20 days of evidence, including from shaken NSW Health staff, Walker handed down his report on 14 August 2020.

Walker found that the state's health department was responsible for serious, inexcusable and inexplicable mistakes. Those failures, though, came from decisions made by medical experts rather than political leaders, which took much of the heat away from Berejiklian's government. However, one of Walker's harshest criticisms was directed at the federal government. Walker said many people were of 'great assistance' during the inquiry, including the New South Wales police commissioner, but the 'one fly in the ointment . . . is the stance of the Commonwealth'. His report said: 'A summons to a Commonwealth officer to attend and give evidence about the grant of pratique for the *Ruby Princess* was met with steps towards proceedings in the High Court of Australia. Quite how this met the prime minister's early assurance of full cooperation with the commission escapes me.' Berejiklian, meanwhile, said: 'I now apologise unreservedly to anybody who suffered as a result of the mistakes that were outlined in the report undertaken by individuals within the health department or the health agency.'

The *Ruby Princess* saga was not the only dark spot for the Berejiklian government in the early months of the pandemic. Outbreaks at two Sydney aged care homes, Dorothy Henderson Lodge and Newmarch House, highlighted just how contagious, and deadly, the virus could be, particularly among the elderly. Twenty-five residents died at the two homes. Footage was shown on the nightly news of loved ones stopped from seeing frail family members, who were locked in their rooms. At one stage, out of desperation, Hazzard ordered NSW Health to set up a coffee tent outside one of the aged care homes for the families as they peered in the windows, hoping to catch a glimpse of their sick family members. It was a small gesture, but Hazzard wanted to let the families know that someone cared. New South Wales was eager to point out that aged care homes were the federal government's responsibility. Internally, ministers were scathing of their federal colleagues' handling of the aged care outbreaks. It was just the start of many more points of contention between New South Wales and Canberra.

Early in the pandemic, Berejiklian had very little faith that she could rely on Canberra for critical supplies. Every government in the world was scrambling at the same time to secure gowns, gloves and masks – personal protective equipment (PPE) – to protect frontline health workers.

Berejiklian looked at the items the federal government could provide from the national stockpile. She was shocked. It wasn't nearly enough, not even to meet the state's needs for a week. 'I knew we had to rely on ourselves,' she said. In her view, New South Wales was the state most exposed to COVID-19, as the country's international gateway to the world. She later reflected: 'I felt I was responsible for 8 million citizens, I had to step up and make sure they were covered. If I relied on the national strategy with procurement, how would I know what I would get?'

Hazzard shared Berejiklian's concerns: 'We had no idea what we would get. By the end, we all became experts in New South Wales in procurement from glove sizes to ventilators.' Berejiklian tapped into her contacts. 'We went to business leaders we knew who had links into the various countries where supplies were,' Berejiklian said, without identifying who helped source the PPE that New South Wales would need in the coming months. 'Quietly in the dead of night we had planes arriving from different parts of the world. It was a huge logistical exercise.'

Berejiklian also relied on trusted business contacts for other advice. Atlassian billionaire co-founder Scott Farquhar fed her intelligence from his business contacts overseas, while the former head of the Sydney Olympic bid Rod McGeoch was another trusted source of counsel. Farquhar described Berejiklian as a standout among state leaders because of her willingness to ask the business community what it needed. Her style was one of 'servant leadership', according to Farquhar. He asked her at the start of the pandemic what business could do to help. Farquhar said: 'She thought about it for a while and said, "The best thing you can do is give me a list of what business needs." Her answer was, "What's important for you is important for me."'

Farquhar helped with establishing the early modelling that convinced Berejiklian's specially convened crisis cabinet to move quickly against the virus, and it was also Farquhar who urged the premier to publicise as much data as possible, so the community would understand what was being asked of them. 'Scott Farquhar is a legend,' Berejiklian told *The Weekend Australian*. 'You don't just need to be a health expert to manage a pandemic, you need to be a data expert and know what modelling shows you – and he is amazing. He helped me in the early days of the pandemic with data and managing data.'

Berejiklian had learned two invaluable lessons from the Black Summer. The first was the power of putting all relevant frontline agencies under one roof, reporting to a single figure in charge of overall operations. During the fires it had been Fitzsimmons. For the battle against COVID-19, Berejiklian appointed police commissioner Mick Fuller. Key agencies based themselves at what was known as the State Emergency Operations Centre at Sydney Olympic

Park, west of the CBD, as they had during the fires. It took the health bureaucracy some convincing but after several weeks health public servants capitulated and joined the police, education and transport departments to coordinate the state's response to the virus. A world map showing the march of the virus across continents dominated a wall of computer screens, which once displayed maps of bushfire locations. Rural Fire Service data was replaced with tables of COVID-19 cases, testing tallies and live news feeds.

Despite her early hesitation, Berejiklian learned another key lesson from the fire season she had just navigated – the importance of fronting the TV cameras, day in and day out, with a trusted expert at her side. She took the same approach that she had used with Fitzsimmons: address the issues but leave the details to the experts. Her sidekick this time would be Chief Health Officer Kerry Chant, whose face would soon become almost as well known as the premier's through dozens of daily 8 am media conferences at the operations centre. Chant had been the state's public health officer since 2008, and although she was well versed in speaking at press conferences – she had previously been front and centre in the planning for potential outbreaks of SARS, swine flu and Ebola – facing the cameras every day became a new part of her job description. The no-nonsense Chant became a daily fixture in the lives of the state's people. Berejiklian understood the benefit of their press conferences. She said: 'You only get public confidence if they know what you are doing is based on expert advice. I felt that if I told the public everything I know, they would feel more confident in taking instruction, and following advice. I took a lot of stuff from the experience of the fires.'

At the beginning of the crisis, Berejiklian and her Victorian Labor counterpart Daniel Andrews were largely in lockstep. Just hours before an evening National Cabinet meeting on Sunday 22 March, Berejiklian and Andrews spoke on the phone. The National Cabinet, created to replace the cumbersome Council of Australian Governments, was only nine days old at that stage. Berejiklian and Andrews were worried the other states were not willing to move as fast as their own more populous jurisdictions. They had watched, in horror, as intensive care units in Italy and Spain were being overrun and knew that there were only 2000 ventilators available in Australia. If the virus took hold in Sydney and Melbourne, they feared the state health systems would be overwhelmed. In New South Wales, secret health department modelling showed that the state was facing 25,000 deaths from the virus in the next 12 months if drastic action was not taken. Many thousands of people were expected to be hospitalised. Berejiklian and Andrews feared the federal government was too focused on the economic impacts of the pandemic. The pair decided on a pre-emptive move.

Berejiklian released a surprise statement ahead of the National Cabinet meeting. 'Tonight I will be informing the National Cabinet that New South Wales will proceed to a more comprehensive shutdown of non-essential services. This will take place over the next 48 hours. Supermarkets, petrol stations, pharmacies, convenience stores, freight and logistics, and home delivery will be among the many services that will remain open. Schools will be open tomorrow, though I will have more to say on this issue in the morning.' Andrews' statement was very similar, although it had a more alarming tone than Berejiklian's, warning that more Victorians would die if these steps were not taken. It was around this time that Farquhar told Berejiklian he was pulling his children out of school. Atlassian's global perspective gave him an early insight into how the virus was growing at a frightening pace. Berejiklian and Andrews' intervention forced Morrison's hand, a move that angered him; however, in a late night press conference after the National Cabinet met, the prime minister backed Berejiklian and Andrews' decision. Australia was to go into its first lockdown.

New South Wales had been preparing for a pandemic for almost two decades. In 2003, newly appointed Labor health minister Morris Iemma (who would go on to become premier) held up a mask at a press conference at one of Sydney's major hospitals. Iemma warned that if the deadly SARS outbreak taking hold overseas was not brought under control, everybody would be wearing face coverings in public. At the time, the suggestion of masks seemed extreme. New South Wales' pandemic plan, the one that was dusted off and used for COVID-19, had been developed in preparation for the anticipated arrival of the viral respiratory disease SARS, which had first appeared in southern China in 2002. New South Wales, and Australia, escaped without an outbreak, but it did mean the state had a plan in place when a vastly more deadly respiratory virus managed to find its way there almost 20 years later. Unlike Iemma, however, Berejiklian had to put the plan into action.

Despite the initial alignment between New South Wales and Victoria, state responses differed dramatically. Over the years, New South Wales had invested in local public health units which made the state's secret weapon, its world-leading contact-tracing system, invaluable in its armoury to fight COVID-19. Morrison described his home state's ability to track and trace COVID-19 cases as the 'gold standard' in the country, and said it was significantly more effective than Victoria's version. The other much-lauded tool was the state's QR check-in system, which was initially designed for pubs and restaurants but would later be used everywhere to boost health officials' ability to watch where the virus was spreading. The state's hotel quarantine, run by New South Wales police, also outshone Victoria's system. Most general duties police from stations across Sydney did stints guarding hotel quarantine sites during the first 18 months of the pandemic. Despite one or two suspected leaks from the hotels being used, quarantine was never officially linked to an outbreak in New South Wales.

New South Wales also kept domestic borders open while other states slammed them shut, a point Berejiklian stressed regularly. She made pointed jibes at the other states, particularly at Victoria. Her crisis cabinet colleagues did not like the snarky remarks, acutely aware that New South Wales' fortunes could change at any stage. There were a couple of close calls. A major superspreader event at a pub in southwestern Sydney, seeded when a man from Victoria stopped in at the Crossroads Hotel in Casula for a beer, threatened to change New South Wales' trajectory. That cluster, which saw more than 66 cases, sparked panic that New South Wales was headed for a second long winter lockdown like Victoria. 'Crossroads was really petrifying,' Berejiklian later said. 'But then to get on top of it I thought, "Gee, we really can live with this" . . . it's been painful and scary, but we held our nerve and we kept things open. Had it happened in any other state they would have shut the whole show down.'

Then, as Christmas 2020 was approaching, an outbreak on Sydney's northern beaches resulted in other states pulling up the drawbridges to New South Wales. West Australian Premier Mark McGowan demanded Berejiklian shut down Sydney. 'Stop playing whack-a-mole,' McGowan said, referring to Berejiklian's decision to impose a localised lockdown, rather than a city-wide one, to keep the outbreak contained. But Berejiklian's method worked.

After the hellish year that had faced her government, by early 2021 Berejiklian was lauded in federal political and business circles as the leader who kept the country afloat during its darkest hour outside wartime. In April 2021, the *Australian Financial Review Magazine* had Berejiklian on its cover. The headline was unambiguous and undoubtedly the most memorable of the pandemic: 'The Woman Who Saved Australia'. Wearing a striking white pantsuit from the collection of her friend, fashion designer Carla Zampatti (who had died unexpectedly earlier that month), Berejiklian posed on the leather seats in the New South Wales Legislative Assembly. She looked glamorous, relaxed and happy. In reality, she was antagonistic that day.

Louie Douvis, an award-winning photographer who has worked with every living prime minister, photographed Berejiklian for the cover story. Douvis described it as one of the least enjoyable experiences in his long, distinguished career. Berejiklian objected to the outfit suggested by experienced stylist Virginia van Heythuysen, complaining it did not fit properly and she did not like it, despite it being a Zampatti. Berejiklian's staff tried to engineer a more candid shot, rather than a portrait, insisting that Douvis trail Berejiklian as she was mobbed by fangirls and families at Sydney's Royal Easter Show. Her office wanted Berejiklian captured as the 'People's Premier'. But that idea was not going to work as a photograph for the cover of a high-end glossy magazine. Douvis stuck to the original plan and location – the floor of the New South Wales parliament, which is better known as the Bear Pit because of the unruly behaviour that is often unleashed in the chamber.

Berejiklian did not try to hide her disdain for the media, although it was not always her position. In Opposition she had a healthy respect for journalists and worked the press gallery relentlessly, always pitching potential news stories to highlight Labor's mismanagement of the transport system. She was the most approachable, friendly and conscientious frontbencher. But as she climbed the ranks in government, and particularly once premier, she became deeply cynical of the press – a position her media directors conceded they could not budge. Douvis, who shares a family connection with Berejiklian, did his best to lighten the mood on the day he photographed her.

He told Berejiklian his work experience assistant had insisted on helping with the prestigious shoot even though it was her birthday that day. 'She had nothing better to do,' Douvis joked. Berejiklian found nothing funny about that. 'Don't put words in her mouth,' Berejiklian snarled. The frosty atmosphere did not improve and Berejiklian did not look him in the eye during the shoot. Douvis, who found the acid-tongued Paul Keating easier to work with, said: 'It wasn't my worst experience but it certainly wasn't one of my best. I would say it was down towards the bottom. Earlier in my career it would have really thrown me and the word that just sticks in my mind is prickly.' He also photographed Berejiklian on a chesterfield lounge in the parliament's historic Parkes Room. At the end of the shoot, Berejiklian smiled, unprompted, for the first time in hours and insisted everybody sing happy birthday to Douvis' assistant. Douvis was miffed that he had done his best to create a striking image that made her look stunning, yet Berejiklian was deeply ungrateful.

In his story for the magazine, *Australian Financial Review* political editor Phil Coorey wrote that Farquhar and Business Council of Australia chief Jennifer Westacott recounted to him that Berejiklian was given an 'almost-standing ovation' at a Business Council of Australia dinner, which was attended by many CEOs who had struggled to get a meeting with the Andrews government during the Victorian crisis. Westacott said: 'She didn't shut the whole state down, and she held her ground by not shutting state borders at the drop of a hat. She handled the whole thing with precision, thorough professionalism and a whole sense they had this under control.' The *Australian Financial Review* article raised the ire of several of her cabinet colleagues for her failure to acknowledge the team effort that had been required to pull New South Wales through. And not everyone agreed with her version of events. One senior minister who was closely involved with her government's COVID-19 response said: 'We had to talk her down from the ledge [during the Cross-roads Hotel outbreak] and convince her not to shut the whole place down again. She is reinventing history.'

When then treasurer Dominic Perrottet handed down his pandemic bounceback budget on 22 June 2021, he was full of confidence and bravado. The very first line of his budget speech boasted: 'New South Wales is back.' He used projections that the state would face no further COVID-19 restrictions. The pandemic was seemingly over, at least according to Perrottet and NSW Treasury. Perrottet drew on his favourite Roxette song to finish his speech: 'And this budget gets New South Wales dressed for success.' Later that night, at the traditional post-budget drinks hosted by the treasurer for the press gallery, Berejiklian was relaxed and chatty. At one point, she checked her phone and was alerted to new COVID-19 cases, but she was not concerned; she had full faith in her contact tracers. She continued the light conversation, taking recommendations for television shows outside her usual genre of reality TV (reporters convinced her to try Canadian comedy *Schitt's Creek*) as well as talking about her love of musicals and the new season collection from Australian designer Scanlan Theodore.

Within 24 hours, everything changed. The budget assumptions were thrown upside down as it became apparent that the new Delta variant was making ground in New South Wales. An unvaccinated, non-mask-wearing limousine driver from Bondi who picked up international air crew from Sydney Airport was Australia's patient zero for the Delta outbreak. He had tested positive a week earlier. By the time the budget was released, the so-called Bondi cluster had ballooned to 31 cases, and a major economic handbrake that the state's Treasury had presumed was gone for good – limiting the capacity of indoor and outdoor settings – was back. By Friday of that week, only three days after the budget was handed down, four local government areas in Sydney's eastern suburbs had been placed in lockdown, not that Berejiklian used that term. She insisted on referring to the restrictions as stay-at-home orders, rather than conceding that her state was heading down the same path as Victoria. The next day, greater Sydney joined the city's beachside suburbs for a two-week lockdown. Those two weeks would ultimately become more than 100 days.

Berejiklian resumed her daily live press conferences as soon as the first suburbs were locked down, and just as her early morning media appearances became must-watch viewing during the first wave, 11 am became the new 8 am during the Delta crisis. Kerry Chant was, once more, by Berejiklian's side seven days a week. With a longer lockdown and no real end in sight, the Berejiklian/ Chant show was even more popular than it had been the first time round. Berejiklian and Chant's messaging began with desperate pleas for cooperation to bring down case numbers and stop the spread in the community. They also tried other tactics, such as guest appearances from emergency doctors, the state's chief psychiatrist, paramedics and nurses to bolster their position. But the pressure of this new challenge was obvious, and Delta was clearly a much more difficult beast to tame. Berejiklian's previous clear messaging morphed into at times confusing rhetoric. She took the state through an evolution of the government's outlook at whiplash speed, beginning with deep concern, then calling the situation a national emergency and finally landing on a position where New South Wales would lead the nation in being the first state to live with COVID-19.

From the beginning the highly transmissible Delta variant threatened to overwhelm the state's defences. The new enemy had the ability to skip several steps ahead of New South Wales' much-celebrated contact tracers. There was also another stumbling block. Australia's vaccination rates were too low to protect the country from the new aggressor. Again, another glib line came to haunt Morrison, when he said the vaccine rollout was 'not a race'. Indeed, it proved to be a race in which the federal government significantly lagged.

In mid July, Berejiklian warned: 'Please do not think that the New South Wales government thinks we can live with this when our vaccination rate is only at 9 per cent.' Her comments were deliberately designed to quash reports that some of her ministers were thinking it might be possible to abandon a zero-transmission strategy if case numbers stayed stubborn. 'No country on the planet can live with the Delta variant when our vaccination rates are so low,' Berejiklian added. Using unusually strong language, she said that to attempt to live with the virus at that stage would risk seeing 'thousands and thousands of hospitalisations and deaths'.

By the end of July, Delta had continued its march across Sydney and 12 local government areas in the city's west and southwest had been identified as specific 'areas of concern'. Those areas are the most multicultural in the state, which created an impenetrable problem for the government; many of the ethnic communities simply did not trust the government. Keeping families separated was also a huge challenge. Local community leaders were at a loss as to how to stop young men roaming the streets at night and catching up with family members. Berejiklian understood from her own migrant background how deeply ingrained the culture of regular contact with extended family is in many communities, but any sympathy she may have had did not lessen the government's response. Harsher restrictions were imposed on those 12 areas, including a night-time curfew and exercise bans. Police patrolled the streets and the army was called in to help as well. Sydney became a divided city. The anger was palpable in parts of the city, made worse when Berejiklian initially refused to meet with the mayors of the worst-hit areas.

The indomitable Delta variant changed many things, not least the standing of popular leaders, Berejiklian included. While the shock and uncertainty of 2020 favoured incumbents (with the exception of Donald Trump), impatience, frustration and even despera-tion kicked in with Delta as lockdowns dragged on for months. The goalposts changed along the way. In 2020, New South Wales was riding high thanks to its 'gold standard' contact-tracing ability. In 2021, a combina-tion of complacency and hubris early on, then a sense of policymaking on the run as Delta took charge, started to alter the political landscape. The result saw Berejiklian's popularity take a hit. A Resolve Political Monitor for the *Sydney Morning Herald* showed Berejiklian's preferred-premier ranking had dropped from 55 per cent in July to 48 per cent by late September.

Berejiklian was often pushed on whether she would tighten the lockdown screws further across broader Sydney, but maintained 'we have the harshest lockdown conditions that any state in Australia has seen'. 'The vaccine is our key tool,' she said, which at the time jarred with Morrison's assertion that the lockdown itself was the 'primary tool'. The focus was on Sydney, but regional New South Wales was not spared and also went in and out of restrictions. At one point, the Byron, Tweed and Kempsey local government areas went into a snap lockdown after a vaccinated woman from Sydney's eastern suburbs, working on reality show *I'm a Celebrity . . . Get Me Out of Here!*, broke the rules and went to the pub. She then tested positive for COVID-19.

Berejiklian and Chant were eager for the public to get behind a statewide effort to achieve 6 million jabs (first or second doses) by the end of August, which would equate to half the state's population. The attention also shifted from zero community transmission, an acknowledgement that Delta was always one step ahead and it would be impossible to beat. As the lockdown continued and students stayed learning at home, Berejiklian turned her efforts to finding a way to get Year 12 students back to school. However, her obsession with final-year school students rankled senior bureaucrats in the NSW Department of Education as well as some within her government. While no one doubted that it was important to support Higher School Certificate students, there was a whole cohort of small children who were not learning to read or write. One senior minister explained Berejiklian's bias came from her own experience at school. The final years of high school had been integral to Berejiklian and paved her way to success. She saw the Higher School

Certificate as the making of her. But when it came to a generation of primary school–aged children who were missing out on some of their formative years of school, Berejiklian seemed blinkered.

Despite the federal government's slow procurement of COVID-19 vaccinations, once the jabs became available in New South Wales inoculation was embraced. Berejiklian's government set up mass vaccination hubs to help get large numbers of people jabbed. Student dentists, podiatrists and speech pathologists were brought in to help bolster the vaccine workforce. Berejiklian also dangled a carrot in front of New South Wales residents. She said that once high rates of vaccinations were achieved residents would be rewarded. She promised vaccinated people would soon be back in restaurants, bars and event venues, albeit with some restrictions.

After nine long weeks in lockdown, Berejiklian unveiled a gift for her long-suffering state; but the 'one thing' she'd promised the state as a measure of relief from weeks of progressive screw-tightening was a slight letdown. Even Chant conceded they were taking 'baby steps'. People in the 12 most tightly locked down areas of west and southwest Sydney could picnic for an hour in a park with their household if vaccinated. Elsewhere, people could meet outside in groups of five – again, only if fully jabbed. Behind the scenes, senior ministers were relieved that Berejiklian had steered away from the rumoured green light for appointments for haircuts and leg waxes. But everyone was ultimately focused on New South Wales hitting the 70 per cent double vaccination target for adults, which would unlock a range of freedoms. New South Wales galloped towards that milestone faster than expected, and 11 October was the date set for the unleashing of the first freedoms – with more to follow as vaccination rates increased.

At that stage, nobody would have predicted that the woman who saved Australia would no longer be in the top job to celebrate when the long winter lockdown finally ended.

9

ICAC AND THE 'LOVE CIRCLE'

ON THE OUTSKIRTS OF WAGGA WAGGA, IN AN UNREMARK-
able industrial estate, is a gun club and a function centre
aptly named The Range. On one side of the site is a
truck smash repair yard; on the other, sprawling land
with shooting ranges. You would be hard pressed to find
a less picturesque area in the historic Riverina town. In
the middle of the site, next to the 1000-person conven-
tion centre, is the headquarters of the Australian Clay
Target Association. The club, which has about 13,000
paid-up shooters, stumbled upon Wagga Wagga when it
was scouting for locations around the country for its new
national head office. The City of Wagga Wagga council
offered to sell the association a block of land for just $1
and the club built its long-awaited headquarters, opening

the same year as the Sydney Olympics. The patron of the club is National Party heavyweight and popular former federal member for Riverina, Kay Hull. But the little-known gun club made a wider name for itself when it took centre stage in Berejiklian's corruption inquiry.

A decade after arriving in Wagga Wagga, the club wanted to expand and started lobbying the New South Wales government, via their dogged local MP Daryl Maguire, for funding to upgrade the clubhouse and to build The Range – which would be used for everything from school formals to weddings and business expos – next door. Only days into the new year in 2017, while most people were still in a post-Christmas slump, Maguire sent out a media release announcing that after years of nagging his colleagues, he had managed to secure $5.5 million from his government for the function centre. Given the state government oversees a $100 billion annual budget, a $5 million grant is, by all accounts, small beer. Nonethe-less, the gun club grant and a $20 million grant for the Riverina Conservatorium of Music in Maguire's home town would become 'case studies' in the ICAC's probe into whether Berejiklian had knowingly engaged in, or encouraged, corrupt conduct during her secret love affair with Maguire.

The investigation into those case studies ultimately ended Berejiklian's premiership. Once the ICAC announced on 1 October 2021 that it had turned its attention to Berejiklian, she immediately stepped down. Despite her protestations of innocence and denials of any wrongdoing, Berejiklian knew all too well that, as a matter of optics, she could not lead the state while under the glare of a corruption probe.

As premier, Berejiklian had been locked in an ongoing battle with the ICAC over its funding, which prompted the commission to seek legal advice from Bret Walker SC – the barrister of choice for politicians, bikies, sports stars and Cardinal George Pell – to bolster its argument.

The ICAC had long been pushing for its funding to be overhauled so it did not have to go cap in hand to the premier's office each time it needed more cash. Walker's view backed the ICAC's position. He concluded that mechanisms where the government of the day is responsible for handing out public money to the very body tasked to investigate potentially corrupt MPs, ministers and premiers were 'undesirable – unlawful, as I see them – aspects of the current funding arrangements for ICAC'.

That was not the only critical report involving the New South Wales government that Walker penned in 2020. He also delivered a scathing response to his special commission of inquiry into the *Ruby Princess* debacle, where he outlined a range of significant mistakes made by NSW Health in the early days of the COVID-19 pandemic. Nevertheless, when Berejiklian's time came to appear again before the ICAC in 2021, not as a witness this time but as the main game, she retained Walker as her barrister. (Berejiklian's previous lawyer, Arthur Moses, could no longer act for her because the pair began dating after her first ICAC appearance.) Walker, who is rumoured to command $25,000 a day in fees, led Berejiklian's legal team, along with Sophie Callan SC, who had just finished prosecuting corrupt former Labor ministers Eddie Obeid and Ian Macdonald over a dodgy coal exploration tender that saw the Obeid family receive a $30 million windfall. Obeid and Macdonald were jailed.

The meticulous and at times disarming barrister Scott Robertson was counsel assisting the ICAC commissioner Ruth McColl SC in the first round of the 2020 investigations into Maguire – Operation Keppel. McColl, a former Court of Appeal judge and defamation expert, was called in as a temporary commissioner to avoid any perceived conflicts of interest for the existing commissioners.

Robertson kicked off the high-stakes inquiry into Berejiklian on 18 October 2021 – just a little over a fortnight after her shock resignation as premier. At the centre of the probe was whether she had breached public trust by failing to disclose her five-year relationship with Maguire. Berejiklian's demise was still raw for many of her inner circle and they were watching the proceedings with acute interest. Supporters and former colleagues of Berejiklian publicly and privately warned that the anti-corruption commission would need some explosive allegations against the hugely popular former premier or it risked a public backlash. Robertson began with a very pointed opening statement. 'Ordinarily, it is entirely a matter for the parties to a relationship to decide whether they disclose the existence of that relationship to anyone and, if so, to whom. However, there are circumstances in which a person's ordinary entitlement to privacy must be subordinated to their public duty. Put in another way, public duties come first.'

Berejiklian was known as a stickler for rules. Robertson deliberately highlighted that in 2013, when she was transport minister, Berejiklian alerted her cabinet colleagues to a possible conflict of interest around the appointment of someone to a government board, and excused herself from discussions. The pair had crossed paths at functions. In 2017, Berejiklian made a confidential disclosure under the NSW Ministerial Code of Conduct because two of her first cousins were employed in the state's public service. And in 2018 Berejiklian noted a possible issue because a person sympathetic to the Liberal Party was hoping to secure a seat on a government advisory board. Yet, as Robertson stressed: 'So far as the material presently available to this commission reveals, Ms Berejiklian never gave a disclosure under the NSW Ministerial Code of Conduct in relation to Mr Maguire.' It seemed a secret romance, even with one of her own, was not worthy of a mention.

Robertson wrapped up his opening address with unambiguous lines, quoting Berejiklian's own set of rules. He said it was essential that 'ministers exhibit and be seen to exhibit the highest standards of probity in the exercise of their offices' and pursued the interests of taxpayers above all else. 'This public inquiry will investigate whether Ms Berejiklian exhibited those high standards of probity that she set for herself and her ministers,' Robertson said.

Berejiklian made much of the importance of her ministers not just doing the right thing, but being seen to do it. As the first wave of COVID-19 was gathering pace in Sydney and the city had been plunged into its first lockdown, Don Harwin, Berejiklian's close factional ally who she had rewarded with a ministry for his years of loyalty, was accused of breaching COVID-19 isolation rules. The then arts minister was hit with a $1000 fine after it emerged that he had been commuting between his inner Sydney apartment and his Pearl Beach holiday home on the New South Wales Central Coast. Sydney-siders were being told they were not allowed to visit family in the regions, yet Harwin seemed to be zipping between homes. Rather than create a problem for Berejiklian, Harwin fell on his sword and resigned from cabinet and his beloved arts portfolio. Harwin always proclaimed his innocence, insisting he did not break the rules, and challenged the fine through the local courts. The fine was ultimately withdrawn and Harwin triumphantly returned to cabinet. Berejiklian said he had done the right thing – quit when he was fined – but it was appropriate for him to go back to his old job once he had been cleared. Perception in politics was everything.

The former premier was not there in person on the first day of the corruption inquiry into her conduct as Robertson painstakingly laid out the ICAC's case against her. But within minutes her voice reverberated around the hearing room as Robertson played a video recording from a secret grilling he had put her through a month earlier. It made for uncomfortable viewing. The private interview was held on a Saturday. Seated at her board-room table in her Martin Place office, with Walker by her side, Berejiklian was reminded by Robertson, via video link, that in July 2018 she was the one demanding Maguire's resignation.

At the time, Berejiklian publicly rounded on Maguire and issued a stern statement: 'I was shocked by the events of Friday and I spoke to Mr Maguire late that afternoon to express in the strongest possible terms my deep disappointment. He has let down his constituents, the people of New South Wales and the New South Wales Liberal Party. Whilst it is for Mr Maguire alone to determine whether he stays on as the elected member until next March, I would encourage him to think carefully as to whether he can effectively represent the people of Wagga Wagga from here on in.' Still she had not told a soul – at least no one in her government, her party or officialdom – about their secret.

So, in the private hearing, being replayed in public, Robertson asked Berejiklian: when did she start to suspect that Maguire might have been involved in corrupt conduct? A flustered-sounding Berejiklian deflected Robertson's questions: 'I was in shock. I didn't know what to think . . . I hadn't read what was happening. I can't remember what I thought at that time. I didn't know, I couldn't make any assumption at that stage. He was professing his innocence and saying it was a misunderstanding.' A clearly frustrated Robertson repeated the question at least four times, stressing he did not want to know whether she *knew* about corrupt conduct but if she had suspicions. 'No,' Berejiklian eventually answered. Robertson's line of questioning was clear. Should the ICAC accept Berejiklian's evidence that she didn't have any misgivings about her boyfriend's dodgy behaviour? Because if she did, Berejiklian had a legal obligation to report it.

The star witness on the first day of the inquiry into the ex-premier's conduct was brutal in his assessment of the worthiness of the gun club grant. A long-time bureaucrat in the NSW Office of Sport, Michael Toohey was the archetypal public servant: sober, stolid and methodical. He revealed that in late 2016 he received a one-line email from his department boss. 'Fancy a challenge?' Toohey's task was to pull together a grant submission for the sports minister Stuart Ayres to take to the expenditure review committee – a powerful subcommittee of cabinet that is chaired by the treasurer of the day, who at the time was Berejiklian. When he later appeared as a witness, Ayres told the ICAC that he thought the function centre proposal had plenty of merit, so much so he signed off on a $40,000 payment to help the gun club prepare a business case. He also conceded Berejiklian perhaps should have declared her relationship with Maguire.

Toohey's boss told him that the project was time critical and the submission was needed that same day – a strange request that the experienced bureaucrat had never before received. 'Extremely unusual,' Toohey described the urgency in his evidence to the ICAC. The submission was for a $5.5 million grant for the gun club. 'What was the rush? Why couldn't it wait . . . I didn't know why it was urgent,' Toohey told the commission. 'Why spend the money on this?' He described the business case attached to the grant application as 'flimsy' and 'deficient' and he could not fathom how the Wagga Wagga economy would benefit from the project.

Toohey outlined in scrupulous detail the curious case of the grant, including discrediting 'imaginative' claims that a new function centre would help secure the state's bid to host the 2018 Invictus Games – an international sporting event for sick, wounded and injured servicemen and women. Fanciful, Toohey thought, because the games do not have shooting events. Most telling, however, was Toohey's assessment of Berejiklian's relationship with Maguire.

Robertson, in his characteristic monotone, asked Toohey: had he known about their relationship, would he have done anything differently? Toohey's response: 'Absolutely.' He said he would have raised his concerns with Ayres' office, probably the Department of Premier and Cabinet and, all else failing, he would have reported it to the ICAC. 'Why were we pushing a grant, an allocation of funds through to a local member based on such scant and inadequate information that didn't meet the NSW Government's own standards and to someone that was in a personal relationship with the treasurer?' Toohey said. 'I can't see how that's anything but a conflict of interest.'

Toohey wasn't alone. Nigel Blunden, the straight-talking adviser to then premier Mike Baird, was also on the ICAC witness list. The ex–Nine Network reporter, who had also honed his political skills working for former Howard government ministers Brendan Nelson and Joe Hockey, did not try to hide his frustration with the handling of the gun club grant. A chain of emails Blunden sent to his boss in December 2016 clearly showed his concerns about what he saw as a half-baked proposal.

Referencing the 1983 film *Risky Business* and the character – played by Tom Cruise – who shacks up with a sex worker and runs a brothel out of his home, Blunden

headed one memo: 'As Joel Goodsen would say, sometimes you gotta say WTF.' A series of emails revealed
Blunden tried behind the scenes to get the gun club taken
off the expenditure review committee agenda, but 'Daryl
fired up and Gladys wanted it put back on . . . Gladys and
Ayres want it,' he wrote to Baird. 'No doubt they're [sic]
done a sweetheart deal with Daryl but this goes against
all of the principles of sound economic management.'
Blunden also jokingly referred to the proposed shooting
complex as the 'Maguire International Shooting Centre
of Excellence' in a briefing to Baird. Blunden told his boss
that the proposal should not be approved without strin-
gent new conditions, including a properly constructed
business case and a benefit-to-cost analysis. His memo
finished: 'Maybe if we make Wagga the world centre for
clay shooting, we can take back that money we wasted on
[redacted].' The redacted section Blunden was referring
to was Berejiklian's pet project, Sydney's light rail.

Baird and Berejiklian had been good friends for many
years. Baird arrived in Macquarie Street as the new MP
for Manly four years after Berejiklian was elected to
parliament. The Liberals were still in Opposition, after
a disappointing election loss in 2007, and the pair hit it
off. Baird, like many of Berejiklian's colleagues, said she
was always warm and caring towards him. He described
her as one of his closest friends in parliament. After
giving up the premiership for him, Berejiklian later

stepped up to be his deputy leader when Baird replaced O'Farrell as premier in 2014. And Baird handed on the leadership baton to his friend when he stepped down as premier in 2017. Baird was always one of Berejiklian's fiercest supporters until her hidden truths were uncovered. Privately, Baird told friends and former colleagues that he believed Berejiklian should have resigned when the ICAC first revealed her clandestine relationship with Maguire a year earlier. To make matters worse, Baird, by then head of a major aged care provider, had to appear before the ICAC to give evidence about his friend.

Baird did not mince his words when he was under oath before the ICAC. The former banker was uncharacteristically terse when asked if he was shocked to discover Berejiklian had been dating Maguire for five years. 'I think incredulous,' he responded. Baird told the hearing he had no idea Berejiklian had been in a 'close personal relationship' with Maguire until it was revealed publicly in 2020. He insisted the relationship between the two should have been disclosed to him as the premier but conceded that Berejiklian never appeared to show any favouritism towards her boyfriend.

But that was not the point for Baird. 'Executing public function in the context of potential private interest, I think in terms of good practice, it should be disclosed,' Baird said. He could not fathom why Berejiklian did not confide in him because they could have managed any potential conflict. Baird also made it clear that he was no fan of Berejiklian's love interest, acknowledging that while MPs always wanted funding for projects in their electorates, Maguire – in Baird's words – could be aggressive, abusive and relentless in pursuing his agenda.

Speaking to reporters outside the ICAC after concluding his evidence, Baird revealed how it felt to publicly admonish a person he still regarded as a close personal friend. 'I'm devastated to be here,' he said. He stressed Berejiklian 'absolutely had the capacity' to manage a conflict of interest, if she had simply told him about Maguire. Baird's evidence ended their friendship. Despite several attempts in the months after to connect with Berejiklian and rebuild their relationship, Baird says Berejiklian ignored him. He was deeply hurt that she had cut him off. 'Gladys and I were very close friends. We really enjoyed working together and I remain very proud of all we achieved. As to recent events, I find it hurtful but will always be open to continuing our friendship,' Baird said, though that seems unlikely.

The friendship with Baird was not the only one Berejiklian terminated. She stopped talking to another long-term political ally and close confidant Rob Stokes, a clean-cut Christian surfer from Sydney's northern beaches, after he confronted Berejiklian about the ICAC rumours in the lead up to her resignation. The pair had been close for many years, as well as serving in cabinet together, and Stokes felt he had a duty to be upfront with her. Once, several years earlier, he was asked in an interview to identify what annoyed him about Berejiklian. Liberal elder and Health Minister Brad Hazzard was also quizzed, and he identified her stubbornness, while the perennially late Perrottet said she was 'always so punctual'. Stokes declared 'nothing' irritated him about his leader. 'No one can hold a candle to Gladys in terms of her intellect, in terms of her capacity, she's just extraordinary,' he said at the time. 'Certainly, she is the smartest person in any room she walks into, that is very clear.'

Stokes' glowing endorsement shifted, however, as the shadow of another ICAC inquiry hung ominously over the government. In the final weeks of her reign, he asked for a formal meeting with the premier, believing he should tell her about the leadership rumblings. He also wanted her to be honest with their colleagues about whether they had anything to worry about. When Stokes went to discuss his concerns about a possible ICAC investigation into her conduct, he was blunt. Stokes told her: 'People are talking and they are talking about leadership,' referring to her jittery colleagues who were on tenterhooks as the rumours swirled. Berejiklian shot back: 'Who?' Stokes responded: 'The people you would expect,' before naming a few colleagues, a choice he later regretted for betraying confidences.

Berejiklian's version, as she relayed to a colleague, was that Stokes had told her that he and his wife were worried about her future, and were praying for her. Berejiklian did not appreciate his meddling nor his sentiment. She also wondered about Stokes' motives, given he had long been touted as a potential leader. The meeting was brief and Berejiklian was defensive. She told Stokes that the government had weathered storms before and would again. Stokes left knowing he had infuriated her and suspected his actions could prove damaging to their friendship. Stokes' intuition was spot on. She was furious at his intervention. Berejiklian also stopped speaking to Stokes.

No one was surprised to see John Barilaro's name on the ICAC witness list given he seemed to have the inside running on the investigation into Berejiklian. By the time the premier and deputy premier had parted ways, there was no love lost between them and there was trepidation within Berejiklian's camp about what the former Nationals leader might say in the witness box. There was genuine fear that Barilaro would be out to seek revenge. As it turned out, their concerns were largely unfounded, although Barilaro did not shy away from his views on whether Berejiklian needed to declare the relationship. 'I've seen many of us declare conflicts of interest for just knowing someone because we worked with someone or have been in an association with someone, let alone being in a relationship,' he said. Barilaro stressed that she should have not taken part in cabinet discussions about the two projects that Maguire was championing for his electorate. He also gave a frank assessment of Maguire: 'He was a pain in the arse.'

Berejiklian's barrister had ammunition up her sleeve if Barilaro lobbed any grenades. He didn't, but Callan used it anyway. There was an unexpected moment of cross-examination when she probed Barilaro on whether he had declared any of his 'intimate relationships' to Berejiklian when she held the top job. Significantly, Callan didn't ask about 'close personal relationships', which is how Berejiklian defined her love affair with Maguire, but deliberately used the term 'intimate'. Rumours about Barilaro's personal life had been swirling around Macquarie Street for months, if not years.

A rattled Barilaro danced around the question. 'I would have, yes,' he said, pointing out there are requirements to disclose assets connected to family members. Callan pushed on: 'What about any other intimate personal relationships?' In a clumsy response, Barilaro replied: 'That's a hard question because my relationships are with my family.' The questioning went no further, but it was clearly a parting shot from Berejiklian's team. Within months of his resignation from parliament, it emerged that he and his wife of 26 years had separated and Barilaro was dating his former press secretary.

Outside the commission, Barilaro was more forgiving of Berejiklian: 'The issue here is potentially a breach of the ministerial code through a conflict of interest. There is no corruption.' Corruption, however, has a broad meaning in New South Wales. According to the definition in the *Independent Commission Against Corruption Act 1988*, corruption can involve bribery, blackmail, tax evasion, illegal drug dealings, harbouring criminals and even treason. However, a less juicy part of the act's definition is 'any conduct of a public official that constitutes or involves the dishonest or partial exercise of any of his or her official functions' and 'any conduct of a public official or former public official that constitutes or involves a breach of public trust'.

Just as Baird loathed being called before the anti-corruption commission to be quizzed about his friend, so did Berejiklian's most trusted employee, her former chief of staff Sarah Cruickshank. The respected public servant, who herself had weighed up a career in federal politics, was seconded from the public service to Berejiklian's office when Berejiklian became premier. The pair had been friends for years, working their way up through the Young Liberals and socialising together. After helping Berejiklian to be reelected in 2019, Cruickshank decided to go back to a senior role in the bureaucracy.

Not surprisingly, Cruickshank was uncomfortable having to appear before the anti-corruption commission to publicly reveal that Berejiklian was not honest with her about the status of her romance with Maguire. The evening after details of Maguire's dodgy dealings were first publicly aired on Friday 13 July 2018, Cruickshank was out at dinner when Berejiklian asked her to call urgently. The workaholic Berejiklian was on a rare break but the premier needed to tell Cruickshank about a 'historic' relationship with Maguire. Cruickshank was shocked by the revelation and Berejiklian seemed shaken.

Cruickshank was 'very surprised and slightly mortified' after their call because she had 'given some free character assessments' about Maguire after his ICAC appearance. As Cruickshank recalled, Berejiklian's main worry was that people may have seen her out with Maguire and would join the dots; or, worse, produce photos of them together. 'I left the conversation with the impression it was more than just a few dinners. I didn't get the sense it was a full-blown intense relationship,' Cruickshank said, adding that she found the whole situation awkward to talk about in a public arena. Berejiklian also stopped speaking to Cruickshank after her appearance at the anti-corruption commission.

Berejiklian's colleagues and staff members were left having to balance their experiences working with the premier with the stunning new information that had come out as a result of the inquiry. Berejiklian and Maguire loved each other. They talked about marriage and having a child together. They went on holidays and Maguire had a key to Berejiklian's house to use when he was in Sydney. Yet still, no one ever caught wind of their romance. After Berejiklian took over as premier from Baird, Cruickshank and the state's then police commissioner Mick Fuller insisted on boosting the security of her townhouse, where she lived alone on Sydney's lower north shore. CCTV was installed at her home and a police officer was parked outside every night. A large metal fence still towers over the property. Compared to the other houses on her street, it is almost Fort Knox and the security was much tighter than other premiers would have experienced. Yet despite the focus on ensuring no one could access the modest three-bedroom townhouse, Maguire was seemingly able to come and go. Even Cruickshank did not have a key.

Intercepted phone calls, text messages and emails played to the anti-corruption commission, as well as his evidence, revealed Maguire's version of the 'close personal relationship' that he shared with Berejiklian. 'You loved her?' Robertson asked when Maguire was called back to the ICAC. 'Yes,' Maguire said.

Robertson: 'And so far as you can ascertain, she loved you as well?'

Maguire: 'Yes.'

Giving his evidence via video link, Berejiklian's former flame told the ICAC that while the pair planned for a future together after his retirement from politics, they never met each other's families. And despite their love, Berejiklian was not spared from his unorthodox ways of getting what he wanted. Maguire described himself as a 'serial pest' and a 'pain in the arse' when it came to lobbying for projects in his electorate. The pair tried to keep their 'private' discussions and 'business' discussions separate, Maguire said, 'but, yeah I would have given her a hard time on certain things. She wouldn't cut any slack.'

When it came to Maguire's persistence, the $5.5 million gun club grant was a case in point. The funding for the gun club was stalled until Maguire took control of the situation. In its 2017 annual report, the Australian Clay Target Association detailed how it had faced a string of rejections before finally getting the cash once Maguire stepped in. 'We must recognise the efforts of Daryl Maguire, the local state LNP member, without whom the project would never have been possible,' the club's report said. Kay Hull, the much-respected former federal member and patron of the gun club, said the association 'absolutely deserved that funding'. 'That grant came about because of the hardworking volunteers,' Hull later said. Maguire was adamant he had nothing to gain from securing the grant, even though his business partner helped the shooting association import a shipping container of furniture from China. Maguire denied he had anything to do with the furniture deal but acknowledged his business partner may have received a cut. 'No one works for nothing, Mr Robertson,' Maguire told the ICAC.

Hull, who was the driving force behind enticing the Australian Clay Target Association to the Riverina back in the 1990s, does not forgive Maguire for any of his questionable business interests that landed him before the anti-corruption commission. But the federal president of the National Party was furious that the reputation of her city had been tarnished – not by Maguire, but by the ICAC and Sydney-based public servants. 'Wagga became a scapegoat and I find it so insulting that those bureaucrats said over and over that we were not worthy of these grants,' Hull said. 'We were not recipients of something we didn't deserve. We absolutely deserved funding, the volunteers deserved the funding, and I truly believe the ICAC has conflated the issues of Daryl's business dealings and grants which is just so unfair. Our city has been denigrated and linked to scandalous grants, which they simply were not.'

Hull is also an avid supporter of the arts community in Wagga Wagga, which she said had been crying out for a new home for many years. While the gun club secured its funding, the full money promised for the Riverina Conservatorium of Music never eventuated. 'The conservatorium will never get funding now, not after the unfair treatment it received. Why should our community be raped and pillaged over a relationship we did not know about, or one that we had no say over whether it was declared. It is unquestionable that we deserved that funding and the conservatorium was a project with absolute merit.'

Berejiklian's much-anticipated grilling came on 29 October 2021, just under a month after her resignation. She arrived at the ICAC's Sydney CBD headquarters looking confident and smiling for the cameras. Callan was by her side. The security detail she had as premier was still with her, along with her former media director Sean Berry. She walked through the throngs of media and uniformed police before delivering the daily catchcry from her COVID-19 press conferences. 'Can I just say, good morning everybody,' she said to the cameras before heading inside.

Robertson was straight down to business once she was on the witness stand. If Berejiklian had her time over, would she have told colleagues about her romance with Maguire? The famously stubborn former premier was clearly not going to budge. 'No,' she replied, without hesitation. No matter how many times Robertson came back to that question over the next few hours, she never changed her position. She was also adamant that the man she hoped to marry one day had not enjoyed any better access or found greater favour with her – consciously or unconsciously – than other MPs or colleagues. She treated them all the same, she insisted. 'All my colleagues had equal access in relation to matters regarding their electorate,' Berejiklian told the ICAC.

She did, however, tie herself in knots trying to explain why their relationship was not 'significant' enough to declare, despite the code of conduct that requires ministers to put on record personal interests, including non-pecuniary interests, that could have an impact on their ability to impartially perform their duty. Berejiklian said she had doubted Maguire's commitment to her, and had not deemed their relationship worthy of revealing to her parents or sisters, despite their talk of marriage and a child. They lived 'very separate lives', she said. 'I never regarded him as family in terms of the ministerial code.' Rather, Maguire was part of her 'love circle', which included 'people that I strongly cared for'. Berejiklian was shown a 2017 text message, in which she told Maguire: 'But you are my family.' She was quizzed on whether that message indicated she did in fact regard Maguire as part of her family, to which she responded 'in terms of my feelings but definitely not in any legal sense'. Robertson shot back: 'We'll let the lawyers argue about the law.' It was one of several moments during her evidence when Robertson, or the assistant commissioner, chastised Berejiklian for her responses. McColl directed Berejiklian to not only answer the questions but to 'stop making speeches'. Berejiklian told the ICAC that she did not want to downplay the feelings that she had for Maguire, but she never felt the relationship was at a stage where she would introduce him to anyone. Colleagues were convinced that she was too embarrassed to admit that she was dating someone who was often the butt of their jokes. Her parents would have also been a major factor: they desperately hoped their daughter would meet an Armenian man. Nonetheless, Berejiklian confirmed Maguire had a key to her house during their years-long romance, but she did not ask for it back when they split. Instead, she changed the locks.

Berejiklian said Maguire pushed for projects in his electorate in 'exactly the same way' as other MPs. He would lobby her directly about proposals in his electorate, but 'so would all my other colleagues'. 'I was always able to distinguish between my private life and my public responsibilities,' Berejiklian said. Berejiklian did not accept that alarm bells should have sounded for her when Maguire spoke about his involvement with property projects hundreds of kilometres from his electorate, such as Badgerys Creek in Sydney's outer west, or Canterbury in Sydney's inner west. Maguire told her he had done nothing wrong and Berejiklian trusted him.

In one intercepted call played before the ICAC, Berejiklian promised her boyfriend that she would step in to ensure $170 million would be delivered for his electorate. In a phone call on 16 May 2018, Maguire whinged about the lack of funding for infrastructure in Wagga Wagga in the upcoming state budget. Maguire warned Berejiklian that then treasurer Dominic Perrottet would have a f..king riot on [his] hands' if projects like the Wagga Wagga Base Hospital and Tumut Hospital were not funded. In a call just hours later, Berejiklian placated Maguire. 'I've already got you the Wagga hospital. I just spoke to Dom [Perrottet] . . . he does what I ask him to. We're giving Wagga more money than ever before. I've now got you the one hundred and seventy mill in five minutes . . . you can't tell me you've been hard done by,' she said. The airing of that conversation did not seem to trouble Berejiklian. A hospital project, she said, would hardly create a conflict of interest for her unless there was some kind of 'private personal benefit'. 'Building a hospital is not a personal benefit to me. It is a community asset,' Berejiklian told the ICAC.

In another tapped phone call, Maguire was heard moaning to Berejiklian that he was in debt to the tune of $1.5 million. 'I am poor, I'm telling you, 1.59 million poor,' Maguire said in the phone call on 1 September 2017. 'Just repeat after me: 1.5 million.' In a subsequent call that month, he told her that a Badgerys Creek land deal would result in him being 'debt free'. Asked if that piece of news raised any suspicions of corruption, Berejiklian said it didn't. 'He was always talking big and I didn't pay much attention to that. I never thought he was doing anything untoward.' Pressed on whether it did not at least strike her as 'strange' that an MP could have made $1.5 million, she said she did not take it seriously. 'I don't even know if I listened properly. He was always talking about pie-in-the-sky things.' Maguire said he often discussed his debts and how important wiping them would be to their future together.

When questioning moved to the controversial multimillion-dollar grant to the gun club in Maguire's electorate in 2017, Berejiklian said it was a project she considered necessary in the context of a recent by-election loss for the Coalition in the seat of Orange. The Nationals were beaten by Shooters, Fishers and Farmers, which saw the minor party win its first lower house seat in New South Wales. 'The bush was on fire in terms of their attitude to the government,' Berejiklian said. 'We'd just lost a seat to the Shooters Party.' Supporting the plan would have 'kept a portion of the community pleased' and the government was keen to show it was not ignoring regional New South Wales.

A second grant that also caught the attention of the anti-corruption commission was for the Riverina Conservatorium of Music, which was given $10 million to move from its old home on a former Charles Sturt University site to a government-owned building. That funding came after vociferous lobbying by Maguire. The conservatorium, which has about 1200 students, was later promised a further $20 million to build a recital hall. When arts minister Don Harwin announced the extra funding for the conservatorium, he boasted: 'By nurturing up-and-coming musical prodigies and providing them with a world-class venue to showcase their talent, we are preparing them for a life on the stage.' The $20 million was never forthcoming.

In a 2017 phone call played to the ICAC, Berejiklian told Maguire of her plan for a bureaucrat she could not 'stand', saying, 'his head will be gone'. Maguire told her that she should not fire him until the bureaucrat finalised the conservatorium proposal. Berejiklian replied: 'Tell him to fix it, and then after he fixes it, I'm sacking him.' Berejiklian never carried out her threat. The bureaucrat was still employed in the public service, she told the ICAC. In a 31 July 2018 email, sent one day after Maguire resigned from parliament, Maguire told the chair of the conservatorium, Andrew Wallace, that the funding had been locked in and he could expect to be part of the by-election campaign. Maguire wrote: 'Ha they got it! My sources just confirmed, stick to the line, you will be ok.' Maguire told the ICAC he could not recall who his source was but when Robertson asked whether it was Berejiklian, Maguire acknowledged it probably was.

Maguire also gave Berejiklian advice on how she should publicly respond to the fallout from his ICAC evidence in 2018, which ultimately ended his career: 'Hawkiss get stuck into me, kick the shit out of me, good for party morale.' Maguire's eventual resignation prompted a by-election in his seat, and the pair's intercepted phone calls reveal he also gave Berejiklian guidance on which projects she should give funds to in order to keep the seat. 'Just throw money at Wagga,' Maguire said in the call on 30 July 2018. 'I'll throw money at Wagga, lots of it, don't you worry about that,' Berejiklian replied.

As she fronted the commission over two days to give evidence about whether she had breached the public's trust through her secret relationship with Maguire, Berejiklian's demeanour said it all. She was defensive and, at times, combative. With the evidence broken up by a weekend, Berejiklian returned after a two-day break even more resolute that she had done nothing wrong. The grants used as the ICAC's 'case studies' did not expose any explosive details and her colleagues were convinced that they were used as a stalking horse to investigate Berejiklian. The former premier repeatedly said she had 'no knowledge' of Maguire doing anything untoward and didn't think she had any information about his business interests that could have helped the ICAC. She also did not back away from her stance that, because of the nature of her 'on-again off-again' romantic relationship with Maguire, there was no need for her to declare it. Clearly agitated, Berejiklian visibly scoffed at some questions and was even dismissive on occasion, leading to some terse exchanges. McColl did not hide the fact that she was unimpressed with Berejiklian's behaviour at times.

The final question to Berejiklian to end the 11-day hearing was: 'You no doubt as a premier and minister attended scores and scores, hundreds and hundreds, perhaps thousands of meetings of cabinet and committees of cabinet. Did it never occur to you during the course of any of those agenda items in those scores or hundreds of meetings, that it may have been desirable, if not required, to make a declaration regarding your relationship with Mr Maguire?'

Berejiklian's answer was simply: 'No.'

10

WHEN THE HALO SLIPS

BEREJIKLIAN'S DEFINING CHARACTERISTICS AS A BOSS were her commitment to the trusted few in her inner circle and her insistence on micromanaging. A long-term senior staff member said Berejiklian always considered her job an honour, and in turn expected her staff to recognise that they were privileged to be working by her side. From her earliest days as a minister, Berejiklian relied on a very small, tight group of people who gave her their undying loyalty, even after they no longer worked for her. In the wake of Berejiklian's resignation, her deputy chief of staff, policy expert and fellow Armenian Arminé Nalbandian posted a glowing tribute to Berejiklian on her LinkedIn account describing Berejiklian as a 'politician we could like'. Nalbandian wrote: 'Throughout the pandemic, she entered our lives and our living rooms, and spoke directly to us. She never stood on ceremony. Gladys told it straight and she did so while leading us through some of our darkest hours as a nation.'

Jonny Heron, who was head of operations in Berejiklian's office, was equally effusive: 'Glad as a friend was, and continues to be, fiercely loyal, caring and great to be around. He described her as a 'thoroughly decent person' and said her office felt like family. He spoke of his time working in Berejiklian's office as 'an honour and privilege that I will never forget'.

Outside her inner sanctum, it seems some staff may have had a different experience; they described working for Berejiklian as like working for the Queen. Berejiklian would walk past them to her office; they would dare not speak to her, and she did not acknowledge them. All communication was made strictly through the exchange of written briefings. 'It's fair to say, only a select few had access to her and I can imagine it would be hard to work for her if you weren't one of those,' an ex-staff member, one of the chosen ones, said. A highly respected former adviser said it could be uncomfortable to witness the way Berejiklian could treat her junior staff, while another said Berejiklian's worst trait was the way she sometimes interacted with some members of her team: 'She was wonderful but could also be terrible.'

Nonetheless, her office ran like a well-oiled machine,

and her staff said Berejiklian signed off on all correspondence in her in-tray, regardless of how insignificant it was. Once, when asked about personally overseeing so much paperwork, she responded that she did not see anything wrong with being across detail. She set the rules early. 'The directive the premier gave was whatever goes out in her name, she has to see,' her office confirmed in the early days of her premiership.

Berejiklian expected her staff to work to her high standards, and they were given firm 'please explains' if correspondence or departmental briefs were not completed swiftly. Staff would fill her in-tray with briefs at the end of each day, and she would stay back in the office until she had worked her way through them all. The next morning her out-tray would be piled high. One former staffer said: 'She was pretty fanatical about never being the cause of any kind of delay. It was exhausting.' Berejiklian always had the television on in her office – sometimes the sound was down, but it was rarely off, even when meetings were underway. It was a quirk that puzzled ministers because it was not news channels she played, but commercial TV or one of her favourite reality shows.

As transport minister, treasurer and later premier, Berejiklian was renowned for her frenetic energy, her ability to exist on very little sleep and her supreme organisational skills. Despite being an avid consumer of reality television, Berejiklian would only indulge in *The Bachelor* or *Keeping Up With the Kardashians* once she was across the next day's agenda. Her discipline also extended to her diet and exercise. While she may have been chubby as a teen, by the time she rose to the highest ranks of elected office, Berejiklian was slim and the gym was crucial to her regime. She would work out at odd hours of the day but made sure she stayed fit.

Her habit of eating a couple of plain Cheds – an Arnott's cracker baked with cheddar and pecorino cheese – for breakfast became a running joke. Berejiklian was often photographed leaving her north shore Sydney home with Cheds in one hand, folders in the other. She did not mind the joke and once tweeted, 'Confirmation: breakfast choice is Cheds not Salada', when some in the media mixed up their crackers. Her office fridge was always stocked with her drink of choice – Coke No Sugar – and she rarely touched alcohol, if necessary nursing a drink all night without taking a sip. Berejiklian made no secret of watching her weight or counting calories. On the election bus during the 2019 state election campaign, journalists were grumbling that the Liberals had failed to provide the customary snacks for travelling media. Embarrassed, Berejiklian's staff promised to remedy the situation and said they would source chips and bottles of water at the next stop. Berejiklian saw this as ridiculous, insisting that the female journalists would be too worried about their waistlines to be interested in snacks.

Early in her premiership, Berejiklian convened a strategy planning meeting and tasked all her ministers with presenting three ideas that they believed the government should pursue. Some turned to their departments for inspiration and guidance, while the more senior or imaginative ministers devised their own. Berejiklian loved some ideas, and loathed others. One that was raised was the Baby Bundle, a $300 pack for all newborns and their families that included, among other things, a change mat, baby wipes and breast pads. The idea came from then treasurer Dominic Perrottet's wife, Helen, who had already had four children by this stage (she went on to have three more). Although initially skeptical, Berejiklian went on to embrace the idea and the popular bag became affectionally known in maternity wards as the 'GladBag'. New mums loved it.

But ministers pointed out that there was only one person in the strategy meeting who failed to suggest a single idea: Berejiklian. Two senior ministers reflected it was emblematic of her leadership. She was a great administrator but lacked vision.

Berejiklian's discipline across all facets of her life was unquestionable. So it was a stark contradiction to her trademark fastidiousness when her handling of a controversial grants program, the Stronger Communities Fund, came under the spotlight in mid 2020, just months before the ICAC investigation revealed her previous close relationship with Daryl Maguire. The premier would not allow letters to school children to leave her office without her tick of approval, yet she did not seem to demand the same level of oversight when it came to a taxpayer-funded grant program. In some cases, letters approving the grants went out on her letterhead, minus her signature, or approvals were done over email.

The controversial Stronger Communities Fund, which came to plague Berejiklian and her government towards the end of her reign, would have been an unremarkable grant program except for the fact that the vast bulk of the $250 million – 96 per cent – went to Coalition-held seats in the lead up to the 2019 state election. Following her predecessor Mike Baird's hugely unpopular decision to merge 44 councils into 20 new ones across the state, Berejiklian's government set up the Stronger Communities Fund to give councils impacted by Baird's amalgamations financial support, including for local projects in their suburbs. Instead, Labor and the Greens labelled it a slush fund for the Coalition to win elections. Once they uncovered the blatant bias in the way the fund was spent, Labor and the Greens pursued the issue mercilessly.

Curiously, the largest benefactor from the program was the blue-ribbon Hornsby Shire Council. That council, in northern Sydney, scored $90 million – well over one-third of the entire fund – to turn a disused quarry into a park, which perplexed many considering the council, in Liberal heartland, was not amalgamated. Hornsby Shire wanted compensation because its council borders shrunk, which meant it lost some rate revenue, and the government obliged, even though that was not the fund's intent. Other big winners were the Dubbo Regional and Northern Beaches councils, both in Coalition seats, which together were given almost $49 million. There was no evidence of a merit assessment or documented rationale for why projects in those council areas were chosen. Berejiklian ticked off on $142 million worth of grants (Deputy Premier John Barilaro about $61 million), but approvals were often in the form of emails from policy advisers that simply said: 'The premier has approved', 'The premier has signed off' or 'DP approval', shorthand for deputy premier approval.

A parliamentary inquiry into pork-barrelling in October 2020, chaired by Greens MP David Shoebridge, heard some extraordinary evidence, including that the $90 million landed in Hornsby Shire Council's bank account within 72 hours and without any application form from the council. Instead, it simply required a couple of phone calls and emails. The shredding of 'working advice notes' within Berejiklian's office was also remarkable, and prompted an investigation by the Information and Privacy Commissioner and the State Archives and Records

Authority. The Information and Privacy Commissioner said the shredding did not breach any laws under its remit, but the State Archives and Records Authority said: 'These working advice notes should not have been destroyed and they should have been retained as state archives.' It did not find, however, that the destruction of documents occurred under 'explicit instruction' by any member of staff. The authority recommended that the government improved how it managed its records.

Berejiklian's former chief of staff Sarah Cruickshank, who by that stage had returned to the public sector in the senior role of a deputy secretary, was called to give evidence to the parliamentary inquiry. She conceded that destroying documents was not how offices should operate. 'As a public servant, I would say I don't think people should be doing that in future,' she said. When pressed on whether it was routine practice to shred notes, Cruickshank responded: 'I would say no, it is not.' Asked later to comment on the State Archives and Records Authority investigation, Berejiklian was quick to point out that its report said the shredding was 'a misunderstanding as opposed to anything systemic or sinister'.

The pork-barrelling parliamentary inquiry, however, delivered a devastating report. 'Ultimately the Coalition designed a scheme with so few checks and balances that $252 million of public money was handed out on a purely political basis to sort out the Coalition's political problems, to gain an advantage in the 2019 state election and to punish any council that had objected to being forcibly merged,' the report, tabled to parliament, said. Berejiklian was unapologetic. Instead, she not only acknowledged that governments buy votes through pork-barrelling, but shrugged her shoulders. 'Guess what? There are more Coalition seats than any other,' she said, which was true, except at the time it held just over 50 per cent of seats. 'Governments in all positions make commitments to the community in order to curry favour. I think that's part of the political process whether we like it or not. The term pork-barrelling is common parlance . . . and it's not something that I know that the community is comfortable with and if that's the accusation made on this occasion . . . well then I'm happy to accept that commentary.'

Liberal upper house MP and committee member Natalie Ward jumped to the government's defence, describing the parliamentary report as 'a biased, partisan sham' and a waste of taxpayers' money. 'There is no attempt at bona fides here on the part of the non-government members, it's just a cheap, political attack by people with no ideas and no vision for New South Wales,' Ward grumbled in a statement. But Ward's words did little to calm some of Berejiklian's colleagues, who were horrified by the premier's brazen admissions about how their government dished out public money.

Some put Berejiklian's words down to a clumsy error or being exhausted after a gruelling couple of years of managing drought, bushfires and then the pandemic. Many suggested the premier was well overdue a break after working around the clock since before Christmas 2019. However, one senior minister said Berejiklian had made it clear to them that it was no mistake. She had meant what she said. Her long-term supporter, senior minister Rob Stokes, was left stunned by Berejiklian's comments. 'I was surprised to learn Glad's comments on pork-barrelling because it was not a practice I thought she'd condone, nor was it consistent with my experience of her,' Stokes later said. Mike Baird was equally perplexed by her comments. 'I didn't agree with those comments but it certainly seems at odds with all my experience with Gladys,' he said. Her successor, Dominic Perrottet, held a similar position, and made his views very clear just weeks after becoming premier. 'Taxpayers expect the distribution of public funds will be fair, I share that expectation,' Perrottet said.

Berejiklian's position on buying votes did not soften. When she appeared at the anti-corruption commission for the second time, Berejiklian told the ICAC that election promises were standard practice. 'Political parties will make announcements based on what they think is going to curry favour with the community,' Berejiklian said. Asked if there was a concern in her office that the

Wagga Wagga by-election was seen as a 'buy-election', she said every by-election raised that concern. 'I don't think it's a surprise to anybody in and around government to know that we threw money at seats in order to keep them,' Berejiklian told the ICAC. Her government spent millions of taxpayer dollars trying to hold on to Wagga Wagga, but even that was not enough and they lost the once-safe Liberal seat to a popular independent.

Perrottet was open with some colleagues that he was gobsmacked at Berejiklian's chutzpah. One of his first tasks just weeks into the premiership was ordering a review of his government's processes for awarding taxpayer-funded grants. He wanted to distance himself from Berejiklian and made it clear that he did not share her acceptance of favouring seats for political gain. As treasurer, Perrottet had been irritated by the amount of money that was spent during the Wagga Wagga by-election (and would have been even more incensed when he heard Berejiklian telling the ICAC that they did it to curry favour).

When the government faced its next by-election, in the Nationals-held seat of Upper Hunter three years later, Perrottet put his foot down and told Barilaro that there would be no cash splash. The by-election was tricky for the Nationals, not only because it was being fought on the future of coalmining in the area but also because the retiring MP had been forced to quit parliament after facing accusations of raping a sex worker – he denied the accusations, and charges were never laid. Regardless, very little was spent on the Upper Hunter by-election and the Nationals retained the seat. Perrottet felt his position on tightening the purse strings was validated.

Just as the upper house inquiry was highly critical of the Stronger Communities Fund, so too was the state's independent auditor-general. In a scathing audit released in February 2022, after Berejiklian was no longer premier, Auditor-General Margaret Crawford said the fund 'lacked integrity'. In her report she highlighted a 2018 briefing note to Berejiklian that said her staff were working to 'get the cash out the door in the most politically advantageous way'. Crawford was highly critical of the motivations for 'setting up these multimillion-dollar grants programs without basic guidelines or record keeping'. Her report said it could have been a 'purposeful attempt to avoid transparency and accountability over the involvement of the former premier and deputy premier [Barilaro] in approving grant allocations'.

Although Berejiklian and Barilaro worked well together at times, they had very little in common other than their migrant backgrounds. Barilaro, a former carpenter who rose to become Nationals leader after edging out his best mate (and godfather to his youngest daughter), Troy Grant, was known for being bombastic. The self-made millionaire with Italian heritage – his first name is Giovanni – was a talented retail politician who at one point fancied himself as a potential deputy prime minister and plotted a move to Canberra. He abandoned that idea when it became apparent he could not win the seat of Eden-Monaro – but not before being quoted calling his then friend and cabinet colleague Andrew Constance, who was considering contesting the seat for the Liberals, a 'c..t' on the front page of Sydney's *Daily Telegraph*. Barilaro and Constance's friendship, as much as such things exist in politics, never recovered.

Barilaro's relationship with Berejiklian did not get off to a great start. After she became premier in 2017, Berejiklian planned the obligatory press conference to announce her new cabinet. Not surprisingly, it is usual for the premier to unveil their new ministry in Sydney, not least so it can be well covered by the metropolitan media. Barilaro, who had been deputy premier for two months before Berejiklian took the top job, insisted on revealing the Nationals' new cabinet positions in his home town of Queanbeyan, near the Australian Capital Territory border. It would have created a strange spectacle of separate announcements, rather than Berejiklian and Barilaro standing together as a united front. But Barilaro would not budge.

In the middle of the night, before the press conferences, Berejiklian decided to bow to Barilaro's demands and texted her then media director Ehssan Veiszadeh at 3.30 am. She apologised for the last-minute change of plans, but asked if they could reschedule her press conference to Queanbeyan. With no time for Berejiklian's office to do the usual venue check before an event, they turned up in Barilaro's electorate and held the press conference in a local park. Waiting for her were a group of protesters, furious at the Coalition government's council amalgamation policy. Berejiklian struggled to make herself heard through the noise of the rowdy protesters and she was forced to detail her new cabinet to the cameras as anti-government placards were waved behind her. She looked flustered. 'Guys, can you just let me finish?' she asked the protesters at one point.

It was not an ideal start for the new Berejiklian/Barilaro partnership, but as a team they often worked constructively over the five years they were in the top jobs. Berejiklian would use Barilaro as a source of counsel, and vice versa. Yet towards the end of their time in parliament, Berejiklian had come to distrust Barilaro and described him privately as a bully. Barilaro was equally critical of Berejiklian and was furious that she survived a scandal that would have ended anyone else's political career.

However, one issue that did not divide them was spending money to save vulnerable seats. While Berejiklian's acceptance of pork-barrelling troubled some of her Liberal colleagues, Barilaro had no such objections. Ahead of the 2019 state election, which saw the

Nationals fighting to retain four of the government's six most marginal seats, Barilaro and his junior Coalition party embarked on the biggest pre-election splurge in the Nationals' history, which included at least $5 billion for major road upgrades, bridge repairs, hospitals, schools and local sporting grounds. Happy to play up his larrikin-from-the-bush persona, Barilaro revelled in handing out cash to electorates that asked for it. He even gave himself a nickname. 'We have been delivering for the regions and that's why people call me Pork Barilaro and I am absolutely happy for them to call me that,' Barilaro said ahead of the 2019 election. He used his self-appointed moniker as much as possible, seeing it as a positive not a negative.

Barilaro was invited to give evidence to the pork-barrelling parliamentary inquiry. Berejiklian had declined to appear – she never saw the grants issue as a scandal, or anything remotely untoward, even sparring with one Sydney newspaper editor over an editorial suggesting otherwise. Like Berejiklian, Barilaro also defended the practice, saying he was 'sick to death of the mistruths spun about pork-barrelling'. 'What we call pork-barrelling is investment . . . I dare you to turn up to these communities and tell them why they don't deserve these projects. When you think about it, every single election that every party goes to, we make commitments. You want to call that pork-barrelling, you want to call that buying votes, it's what the elections are for.'

But as the Wagga Wagga experience had already shown, pork-barrelling was not always the magic bullet. The North Coast electorate of Ballina was a safe Nationals seat until the Greens won it in 2015 amid a wave of opposition to coal seam gas extraction. In 2019, the Nationals were determined to win it back. 'It was like it was raining gold,' was how Ballina Greens MP Tamara Smith described the pre-election promises from the Coalition. Smith easily retained the seat. In the Central West seat of Orange, the government was so desperate to win back the seat it had lost to the Shooters, Fishers and Farmers in a by-election in 2016 that Berejiklian made a conditional promise to build a $25 million stadium. Berejiklian said the stadium would not be built unless Nationals candidate Kate Hazelton was elected. The premier's efforts to buy votes backfired. At the 2019 poll, Shooters MP Philip Donato was not only returned but increased his margin significantly.

In the same month she made her controversial comments supporting pork-barrelling, it emerged Berejiklian had another lapse in judgement: she had broken her own COVID-19 rules. After months of urging the people of New South Wales to 'do the right thing', the premier had to admit she did not practise what she preached. The premier had taken a COVID-19 test but failed to isolate while awaiting her results. At the time, there were strict rules around staying out of contact with others until a negative result was confirmed. Berejiklian and Chief Health Officer Kerry Chant had been at pains to tell the public that anyone with even the slightest of symptoms – even a 'scratchy throat' – must be tested for COVID-19 and, critically, isolate in their home.

As she began to lose her voice, Berejiklian wanted to play it safe and had a COVID-19 test. She had privately told cabinet colleagues earlier in the pandemic that they could receive discreet testing at a Sydney hospital where they would not have to wait in a lengthy queue and would receive fast-tracked results. She had one of those tests, but did not isolate while waiting for the results. The premier ultimately admitted she did the wrong thing but still down-played the offence as something as minor as forgetting to shut a door to stop people coming in and out of her office. 'In hindsight, I should not [have] seen anybody for the 90 minutes to two hours while I was waiting for the result,' she said. 'I didn't change my schedule. Perhaps I should have. But it was only because I was tired and losing my voice and I knew that I didn't have any symptoms.'

Berejiklian was not the first leader who had been criticised for double standards in the pandemic. At the beginning of the outbreak in March 2020, as a shell-shocked Australia was coming to terms with the idea of restrictions being imposed on their lives, Prime Minister Scott Morrison announced that large crowds would be banned from major events within days. Then, without a hint of irony, he declared that he still intended to go to the football to watch his beloved Cronulla-Sutherland Sharks play that evening. Amid the fuss over Berejiklian's failure to follow her own rules and isolate, the ABC's go-to COVID-19 commentator, Dr Norman Swan, was asked by presenter Leigh Sales on 7.30 about politicians or public health officials around the world 'violating the rules that they are asking their own citizens to follow'. Swan responded: 'Trust is a core element here and you risk, as a leader, breaching that trust and people have to rely on leaders to get them through this.' While Berejiklian reluctantly acknowledged her COVID-19 misstep – 'I'm judged accordingly and I have to accept that' – she also sought to downplay it.

At the heart of the anti-corruption commission investigation that ended Berejiklian's career was the relationship between the state's top elected official and Maguire. Just as with the pork-barrelling allegations, the former premier denied all wrongdoing and maintained that she did not need to disclose their relationship because the romance did not pose any conflicts of interest. However, regardless of the result, the ICAC inquiry served a vital public interest in shining a light on the way politicians go about spending public money, and the reasons they do it.

The investigation was also emblematic of the stubbornness and temerity Berejiklian displayed during the latter years of her premiership, even as her halo started to slip.

11

THE NEXT CHAPTER

A DEFIANT BEREJIKLIAN WALKED OUT OF THE ANTI-corruption commission on 1 November 2021 after two days of gruelling evidence looking confident and strong. She reiterated to the waiting press pack that she had done nothing wrong and had only ever put the public at the forefront of all her decisions. With the spectacle of the inquiry behind her, Berejiklian vowed to get on with her life. After her less than edifying appearance before the ICAC, it was hard to know what that life would look like. The inquiry had provided incredible evidence through phone taps of Berejiklian telling her former boyfriend that she would 'throw money' at his electorate of Wagga Wagga and assuring Maguire she had secured $170 million for a new hospital in his electorate in 'five minutes'. A text message was tendered where she said to him, 'You are my family', and she described him as being in her 'love circle'. It was gripping evidence for those who were watching, and there were many. The ICAC would not reveal how many people tuned in to its livestream, but it was enough to make its system crash on the first day that Berejiklian was in the witness box.

However, while the revelations were extraordinary to those paying attention, Berejiklian's halo had not slipped for everyone. A survey conducted by research company Resolve Strategic for the *Sydney Morning Herald* the month after she gave evidence showed Berejiklian's popularity had rebounded after her ICAC appearance. Most people still liked and respected her, and more than 40 per cent of voters did not think she should have resigned based on what emerged from the corruption inquiry. Interestingly, despite her scathing assessment of the anti-corruption commission in her final public statement as premier, 47 per cent of people still felt that 'ICAC has done important work and should not have its powers reduced'. Overall, much of the court of public opinion seemed to think Berejiklian simply had terrible taste in men. Within days of her shock resignation, Berejiklian was already being touted as the Liberals' best hope for the federal seat of Warringah – including by the prime minister.

Scott Morrison had been the state director of the New South Wales division of the Liberal Party when

Berejiklian was elected to parliament in 2003, but the pair were never close. Years later, when Berejiklian was premier and Morrison prime minister, any previous good relations had soured. After the Black Summer bushfires and then the pandemic, Berejiklian confided to her closest colleagues that she felt bullied by Morrison. In September 2021, then New South Wales treasurer Dominic Perrottet was asking the federal government to stump up for more JobKeeper-style funding in the aftermath of the Delta COVID-19 outbreak, which had been particularly damaging for the New South Wales economy. Federal Treasurer Josh Frydenberg was reluctant, to say the least, as was Morrison. The prime minister was also annoyed by Perrottet's public interventions, which included threatening that New South Wales would go it alone if the federal government did not reinstate JobKeeper. Morrison felt Perrottet was undermining his government, leading to an infamous exchange.

On a video hookup at the time, which included Morrison, Frydenberg, Berejiklian and Perrottet, the prime minister told the New South Wales treasurer to 'f..k off'. After the meeting, Berejiklian reassured Perrottet that Morrison often treated her with the same disrespect. In fact, she took such a dim view of Morrison that she bemoaned to some in her inner circle that she wished Peter Dutton had won the leadership ballot in 2018 rather than Morrison. When asked about her views – which had been canvassed by leading political columnists – at one of her 11 am press conferences, Berejiklian took her commonly used approach of criticising the media. 'Don't believe what you read in newspapers,' she shot back.

Despite any bad blood between them, Morrison knew that Berejiklian was very popular and an asset to the Liberal Party, even after she resigned. She would be a boon for his team, if he could twist her arm. Morrison laid the early groundwork on the floor of federal parliament when he issued a stunning denunciation of the ICAC amid its investigation into Berejiklian. Of course, it was not simply about supporting his 'friend' in her time of need. The Morrison government was opposed to a federal integrity commission, and the downfall of the popular premier provided the perfect springboard to resist such a body – a 'kangaroo court', as the prime minister called it. 'These matters should be looking at criminal conduct, not who your boyfriend is,' Morrison boomed in parliament. 'The premier of New South Wales was done over by a bad process, an abuse of process. Criminal conduct is what this should look at, not chasing down peoples' love lives.' As political commentator Katharine Murphy wrote for *The Guardian*, Morrison was hell-bent on rebranding the New South Wales anti-corruption commission as a publicly funded voyeur. 'Gossip Girl Got Gladys' was how Murphy described Morrison's pitch.

As well as wanting to block a federal ICAC, Morrison was running a conscription drive to get high-profile candidates into must-win seats, and top of his list was recapturing Warringah. Tony Abbott's former seat had been snatched from the Liberals by barrister and Winter Olympian bronze medalist turned independent candidate Zali Steggall in 2019, and the Liberals wanted it back. Steggall was also a vocal supporter of a national integrity commission. Former New South Wales premier Mike Baird, a Manly local, was the first recipient of Morrison's overtures. But Baird could not be convinced. After he quit politics, he returned first to the private sector, as a NAB executive, and then became chief executive of aged care provider HammondCare. When his job at the not for profit was announced in April 2020, he said: 'I think I have made my contribution in politics but you never say never, never, never, although I can't see a situation arising where that would change.' Baird's allies are convinced he could still be talked into a federal political career down the track.

With Baird not an option, Morrison pushed for Berejiklian to be his much-needed star recruit. It seemed fanciful from the start, not only because the reason she resigned as premier was because she believed she could not be in public office and under investigation. Over the years she had ruled out going to Canberra, insisting that she did not think she could cut it there. She did not shift from that position. In March 2020, after the horror Black Summer was over and the bushfire recovery was underway, Berejiklian ended simmering speculation among her colleagues and committed to contesting the 2023 state election. 'Nothing I could ever do would be as good as what I am doing. Nothing. Who gets to run the best state in the country? So nothing I will ever do in life professionally will compare to what I am doing now.' Her statement confirming her intention to stick around reassured some of her colleagues but rankled others, because it was the first time she had articulated her leadership timeline plans.

Liberal Party elders, including Tony Abbott, John Howard and Bruce Baird, supported the idea of Berejiklian going into federal politics. Baird's son Mike had told the ICAC that he was 'incredulous' that Berejiklian did not declare her relationship with Maguire, and he agreed it was 'clear that she should have' disclosed the romance but said voters saw it as a relationship between a popular premier and a 'dud bloke'. Baird senior texted Berejiklian and urged her to consider running in Warringah. He said: 'She captured a whole following and it's not easily erased,' although he acknowledged there was some danger if the ICAC's findings turned out to be worse than expected.

Most Liberals were dismissive of that concern, convinced that Berejiklian would only be pinged for not disclosing her relationship and most voters would not care anyway. Finance minister and senior moderate faction member Simon Birmingham told the ABC, 'It's pretty sad when ICACs go out and destroy reputations, do so in pretty murky ways, looking into relationships and other things,' while Jason Falinski, Liberal MP for the neighbouring northern beaches seat of Mackellar, said the party was 'putting Gladys forward' because she had good ideas about jobs, housing affordability and net zero targets. He was insistent that the party was not concerned about repercussions from a possible adverse finding by the ICAC. Falinski said: 'Most people in New South Wales have discounted the ICAC.' Abbott told the *Sydney Morning Herald* Berejiklian's management of COVID-19 made her an ideal candidate for federal politics: 'Gladys did a fine job as premier and was by far the best of them at resisting virus panic and calls for lockdowns. We certainly need more people in Canberra with an instinct for freedom and a feel for small business and it would be good to keep Gladys in our public life.'

Campaigning in the eastern Sydney electorate of Wentworth with Liberal MP Dave Sharma, Morrison furiously endorsed the former premier and blasted the 'shameful' treatment Berejiklian received from the ICAC. 'We've seen, you know, recordings of private conversations, detailed, intimate things that were paraded around in the media. What was that about? Was that about shaming Gladys Berejiklian? I thought that was awful.'

He went further: 'What I found is that Gladys was put in a position of actually having to stand down and there was no findings of anything. Now, I don't call that justice.' He stressed that Berejiklian was 'a person I've always found to be of great integrity' and 'if she wants to have a crack at Warringah for the Liberal Party, I suspect the people in Warringah would welcome that. I'll let the people decide.'

Just days after publicly campaigning for Berejiklian to make the jump to federal politics, Morrison changed his tune and downplayed the chances of it happening. 'That's a decision for Gladys ultimately, and she may choose not to go ahead here, I suspect. That's a matter for her and I respect her choice.' After more than a week of speculation, Berejiklian phoned in to speak to her friend, 2GB breakfast host Ben Fordham, on air to rule out contesting Warringah. Berejiklian told Fordham that she had no intention of returning to politics: 'I won't be contesting the seat of Warringah, or any other seat for that matter. I'm going into another different direction and I'm looking forward to the opportunities next year brings. I'm looking forward to a much less public life.' Her refusal to accept Morrison's none too subtle pleas created a bigger mess for the prime minister. There was now no candidate for the seat. The frontrunner before Morrison's intervention had been young female barrister Jane Buncle, exactly the sort of candidate the Liberals were trying to attract. After the frenzy over Berejiklian,

Buncle pulled the pin and withdrew her nomination for preselection.

Another mishap for the Liberal Party occurred in the months after Berejiklian's political demise. As the media attention shifted to her successor Dominic Perrottet's handling of the summer's Omicron wave of COVID-19, more private details of Berejiklian's life were once again thrust into the public spotlight. It involved text messages, but this time it had nothing to do with the anti-corruption commission. Rather, it was a trusted ally, a 'senior cabinet minister', who had the gall to reveal an exchange they had with Berejiklian. That exchange landed in the hands of political journalist and commentator Peter van Onselen. Van Onselen – who has long ties to the Liberals, including working for Tony Abbott and coauthoring *John Winston Howard: The Biography* – used the televised National Press Club to drop his bombshell. Morrison was giving the Press Club address. Only a week earlier, van Onselen had written a divisive opinion piece for *The Australian* in which he was highly critical of outgoing Australian of the Year Grace Tame for being 'rude and childish' towards Morrison after a frosty face to face at a morning tea just hours before her reign as Australian of the Year was due to end. Van Onselen later conceded the article 'probably' didn't need to be written and he perhaps should have kept his thoughts to himself. Morrison's wife Jenny was also critical of Tame, insisting she should have been more polite when invited into someone else's home (even if that home was The Lodge).

In a question to Morrison, van Onselen revealed to the prime minister that he had been handed a text message exchange from 2019 which, among other things, included Berejiklian describing Morrison as 'a horrible, horrible person' who could not be trusted and bemoaning that he was more concerned with politics than people. The unnamed cabinet minister responded: 'The mob have worked him out and think he's a fraud,' and went a step further in another text calling Morrison a 'complete psycho'. Berejiklian's self-appointed number one backer Matt Kean was immediately fingered as the anonymous minister, though this was never publicly confirmed. Van Onselen said Berejiklian, in another exchange, described feeling 'gutted' at Morrison's handling of the deadly Black Summer bushfires, and she also accused him of 'actively spreading lies' about her. Van Onselen's question to Morrison after his Press Club speech was as surprising as it was damaging to a prime minister languishing in the polls just months out from a federal election.

A clearly stunned Morrison responded to van Onselen's question with: 'I don't know who you're referring to or the basis of what you've put to me. But I obviously don't agree with it, and I don't think that is my record.'

Relations between both leaders' offices had been rocky at various times, starting with the bushfires. Berejiklian had been furious that Morrison's staff seemed responsible for backgrounding against her, especially during Sydney's Delta outbreak. After the Press Club incident, Berejiklian's loyal ex–media director Sean Berry was quick to send out the statement on behalf of his former boss. Berejiklian, a prolific texter who always deletes messages, did not deny sending the texts but said she had 'no recollection of such messages' and insisted Morrison had her 'very strong support'. 'Let me reiterate my very strong support for Prime Minister Morrison and all he is doing for our nation during these very challenging times,' she said in the statement. 'I also strongly believe he is the best person to lead our nation for years to come.'

Berejiklian, a servant of the Liberal Party, would have been deeply uncomfortable with her private conversation being used as ammunition against the prime minister, regardless of her feelings towards him. Worse still, the closed-book former premier would only have been so candid with a few of her closest allies, which is why moderate powerbroker Kean was thrust into the firing line. Kean makes much of the fact that he is Berejiklian's biggest supporter, so to divulge a private text exchange between them would have been audacious. However, his dislike of Morrison is also well known, fuelled in part by Kean's zealous pursuit of climate change policies when he was state environment minister. In January 2020, riding high after making a bold statement (for a Liberal) that climate change was to blame for the orange cloud of bushfire smoke that had choked Sydney the month earlier, Kean publicly warned that Morrison's own cabinet ministers were unhappy with the federal government's environment policies. Morrison slapped Kean down. No one in his federal cabinet would even know who Kean was, Morrison scoffed after Kean's climate criticisms.

The morning after the text leak, Kean gave an awkward radio interview with 2GB's Fordham where he tried desperately to deny any involvement, while also managing to leave some wriggle room. He need not have bothered. Van Onselen later confirmed the text exchange involved a federal minister and the rumour mill went into overdrive, forcing a parade of Canberra ministers to issue denials. One of the most unlikely people in the frame was the no-nonsense foreign minister Marise Payne. Her relationship with Berejiklian stretched back decades to when Payne helped the 20-something up-and-comer win the Young Liberals presidency. 'I can say categorically that these claims have nothing to do with me. I have never had such an exchange with the former premier, nor have I ever used such language, and nor did I like the messages, if indeed they are genuine. It is ludicrous to suggest otherwise,' Payne said.

Several other ministers also released 'not me' statements. The prime minister did his best to shrug off the bitchy texts. 'I'm not fussed,' Morrison said. Without letting on how he could possibly know, Morrison insisted he was confident the culprit was no longer a member of his ministry and he didn't need to discover their identity. Federal Labor, meanwhile, was convinced that the release of historical text messages dating back to the Black Summer bushfires was sanctioned by Berejiklian, on the condition they were used once she was outside politics.

Despite the occasional thrust back into the spotlight, Berejiklian tried to maintain a low profile in her post-politics life. In June 2021 it emerged that she had a new partner: the lawyer who represented her during her first appearance at the anti-corruption commission, high-profile Sydney silk Arthur Moses. Talk of their fledgling romance had been circulating in political and business circles for months but became public when Berejiklian's sister Mary outed the new couple on Instagram. In what was clearly a staged photo on a Friday evening, Berejiklian (who was still premier) and Moses were looking lovingly into each other's eyes in a setting that was more 1970s *Australian Women's Weekly* than a 2021 selfie. Mary captioned it: 'After work Friday feels with these two. Glad and her boo.' Journalists had been asking Berejiklian's office about the rumours that the pair were dating, but had been met with denials (albeit halfhearted) as well as admonishment for intruding on her private life. Eventually, after the couple accepted that the romance would become common knowledge once Berejiklian and Moses were spotted together in public, Mary gave them a helping hand and Berejiklian's secret was out. Berejiklian's media team immediately released an awkwardly worded statement saying: 'They have recently begun spending private time together. The premier will not discuss her private life.' The office later confirmed that Moses was no longer Berejiklian's lawyer.

Moses was largely known as an employment law expert but also represented Victoria Cross medal recipient Ben Roberts-Smith in his multimillion-dollar defamation case against three newspapers over a series of reports he alleged wrongly portrayed him as a war criminal. Moses also had a history of appearing in corruption investigations, including representing deputy senior Crown prosecutor Margaret Cunneen SC in her high-profile case against the ICAC, which was touted as another example of the ICAC's vendetta against the Liberals. (Cunneen has been talked about as a potential candidate for the party.)

Berejiklian's new partner has also had a long involvement with the Liberal Party. Moses had considered a tilt at state politics, and planned to nominate for the northwest Sydney seat of Epping ahead of the 2007 state election, but changed his mind at the last minute. 'In the longer term I would like to consider a career in either federal or state politics, but not just now,' Moses said at the time. A senior New South Wales Liberal said Berejiklian had over the years sought counsel from Moses on policy issues, as well as judicial appointments. 'Gladys has always held a torch for Arthur,' the Liberal said.

Once any further political aspirations were dismissed for Berejiklian, talk was that she would take a lucrative role at Macquarie Bank – however Singtel-owned telco Optus ultimately lured the former premier. Optus chief executive Kelly Bayer Rosmarin, a former Commonwealth Bank executive, praised Berejiklian as a 'gamechanger' in her new role as managing director of enterprise, technology and institutional. 'Gladys is a proven leader who demonstrated her renowned strength, leadership, discipline and composure in successfully guiding Australia's largest state through one of the biggest challenges in its history while earning the support and gratitude of the community for her tireless contribution,' Bayer Rosmarin effused. 'She also builds and fosters loyal and dedicated teams who really go above and beyond for her.' (Even after Berejiklian's political demise left him unemployed, Berry continued to handle her media and was by her side at the ICAC inquiry.)

However, it was hinted that the looming report from the anti-corruption commission could still be an issue for Berejiklian. The same week that Berejiklian started her new job, chair of Optus Paul O'Sullivan was on stage at the Australian Institute of Company Directors' Australian Governance Summit in Melbourne.

O'Sullivan was asked about the telco's decision to hire Berejiklian amid the uncertainty of the ICAC investigation. O'Sullivan sang Berejiklian's praises before adding that the company would have 'to see how ICAC plays out'. Others in the business world were more wary. A long-term political observer who sits on a not-for-profit board said Berejiklian's name was floated as a contender for a director on his board. The advice was to hold fire until the findings of her ICAC investigation were clear.

After her premiership spectacularly imploded, Berejiklian formally resigned as the member for Willoughby, three months short of her 19th anniversary as an MP. Another former minister from her class of 2003, Andrew Constance, also handed in his notice for the South Coast seat of Bega so he could contest the federal election for the Liberals in Gilmore. Barilaro quit politics too, as did the ex–Labor leader Jodi McKay, who had resigned from the top job months earlier after a disastrous showing in the earlier by-election in the Upper Hunter. The resignations forced a Super Saturday of by-elections on the newly minted premier Perrottet. Soon after her resignation, Berejiklian's friend Don Harwin also announced his retirement from parliament. In his valedictory speech to the upper house in March 2022, Harwin said: 'I was pleased and proud to enter the ministry with Gladys Berejiklian as premier, serving as her Leader of the Government in this place. As I always expected would be the case, I finally left that role when she left the premiership. It was just somewhat earlier than she and I had planned.'

Part of the by-election frenzy was the hotly contested preselection in Berejiklian's old seat. Despite Berejiklian only just making it over the line in 2003, over the years that followed she made Willoughby a safe Liberal seat. Vying for a chance to represent Willoughby were three candidates: the mayor Gail Giles-Gidney (Berejiklian's pick), former journalist turned executive Kellie Sloane (who had Joe Hockey's backing) and conservative candidate Tim James (supported by the former member Peter Collins). Normally, James would have been the obvious preference for Perrottet, hailing from his right-wing faction. However, Perrottet's early days in the leadership saw him face criticism for his senior team being too white and too male. Twice in his first week of the job he held press conferences in pubs, surrounded by booze. The intention was to celebrate the opening of the economy after the long Delta lockdown. Instead he made it look like it was beers with the boys without a female to be seen. Perrottet knew he had to fix his blokey image quick smart, so he added one extra woman to his cabinet and hired a female media director (who happened to be Berry's wife, former News Corp reporter Miranda Wood). Perrottet told people close to him that James would not be the right fit to replace a popular progressive woman.

James also had baggage. He had tried to unseat the state member for North Shore Felicity Wilson ahead of the 2019 state election, which created bad blood within the party. Wilson came under pressure over her claims of how long she had lived in her electorate and James did his best to exploit apparent inconsistencies in her preselection application. In the end, Berejiklian staged an unprecedented intervention and wrote to the selection committee, describing Wilson as 'a fighter' and the candidate 'best placed to represent the Liberal Party at the 2019 state election'. 'I am asking directly for your support to ensure Felicity can continue to make a valuable contribution to her constituents and my government,' Berejiklian's letter said. Wilson scraped in and was preselected, although James took Supreme Court action in a bid to overrule his party's decision. He claimed the result was invalid because an unidentified person bypassed identification checks to get inside the preselection event, or someone in the room voted twice in the ballots. James was unsuccessful and Wilson was reelected as the member for North Shore.

Still desperate for a seat in parliament, James pursued preselection in Willoughby when Berejiklian quit and finally he was successful. He beat two women to become the Liberal candidate. Any past animosity was put to the side as Berejiklian, the ever-faithful team player, publicly backed James and urged her electorate to vote for him.

Berejiklian's face was on corflute signs across Willoughby, although she wasn't seen on the hustings with him.

While Bega was seen as at threat for the Liberals, Willoughby should have been a safe bet – except polling even before the election showed the Liberals were in trouble without Berejiklian. James ended up victorious, but was nearly defeated by Larissa Penn, a local mum who ran her campaign with the help of volunteers from the local schools and very little cash. After 18 years, it was back to the future. Willoughby was once again a marginal seat.

Berejiklian spent the final weeks of her political career exactly where it had begun – in her electorate office, as a backbencher, responding to constituents. The once-little-known Armenian head girl was now a household name. When Berejiklian walked out of her office in Willoughby for the final time on 30 December 2021, she did it without fanfare. The no-fuss former premier left a simple handmade poster in the window. It read: 'It has been an honour and privilege to serve our wonderful community for almost 19 years. I will miss everyone.'

Five months later, as the 2022 federal election results began trickling in, Berejiklian must have been relieved that Scott Morrison had not managed to strong-arm her into a tilt at federal politics. Under his watch, voters turned on a party that became defined by its tin ear on climate change, women and integrity in government.

As Berejiklian watched Liberal friends fall, including her long-time ally Trent Zimmerman, six progressive independent women changed the face of Australian politics and helped ensure a change of government.

Former deputy Liberal leader Julie Bishop did not mince her words to Channel Nine on election night when she bemoaned why an Anthony Albanese–led Labor was swept to power. 'Women did not see their concerns and interests reflected in a party led by Scott Morrison in coalition with Barnaby Joyce.' And the result? The House of Representatives is now more representative than it has ever been. Fifty-eight women, including 19 first-term MPs, were elected to the lower house. Women now make up 38 per cent of the chamber in the new parliament, the highest ever proportion on record. Proof of what happens when women are ignored for too long.

For all its highs, lows and contradictions, Berejiklian's career has served as a test case for how women fare at the upper level of politics. Berejiklian was Australia's rockstar premier. She rose to the top of her game against the odds and led New South Wales through devastating bushfires, drought and a once-in-a-generation pandemic. Hard work and grit, rather than privilege or pedigree, saw her leapfrog men (and women) to reach positions that saw her make history. She delivered infrastructure, in spite of fierce opponents, as well as social policy that was driven by her strong, although often-understated, progressiveness. Berejiklian's friends and foes admired her work ethic and unswerving loyalty to her beloved Liberal Party. Her fierce stubbornness was a defining trait, yet the most common word used by her political allies and friends to describe her was 'complex'. In the end, many wondered if they really knew Berejiklian. Her determination to be a squeaky-clean loyal servant to the people of New South Wales, as well as the perfect daughter to devoted migrant parents, meant that she kept her personal life a secret for years, starting even before she became premier. That secret would end the political career of one of the country's most revered leaders. Falling in love with the wrong man was a tragic end for a woman who, while by no means without fault, had achieved so much.

Haig Kayserian, executive director of the Armenian National Committee of Australia and the public voice of Armenians in Australia, was not prepared to accept that this was the final chapter for Berejiklian. Kayserian had cheered on Berejiklian from the very beginning of her career. He was convinced Berejiklian would rise again. 'I don't think her story has been fully told. Not because I have any information. But because I have hope. I think Australia, the Armenian Australian community and the greater world of politics needs Gladys.'

ACKNOWLEDGMENTS

THE IDEA TO WRITE THIS BOOK CAME TO ME AS I WAS locked away from my family in my young daughter's bedroom for a fortnight. It was the very early days of the Delta COVID-19 outbreak in mid 2021, and I was forced to isolate after being classed a close contact. I had plenty of time to think and became convinced that the rise, the fall and the rise again of Gladys Berejiklian was an extraordinary tale. Not surprisingly, it was a trio of amazing women who made this book happen. The ever-generous Jenna Price, who exists almost solely to be a guardian angel for women, hooked me up with my fabulous agent Grace Heifetz, who understood the book immediately. I could not have asked for a better publisher than Cate Blake. Her enthusiasm from the beginning was contagious. My editors, again both female, were so encouraging.

Thank you to my amazing *Sydney Morning Herald* colleagues and fellow political junkies Lucy Cormack and Tom Rabe, who kept me sane during that long fortnight in isolation with their hilarious messages and later their support and suggestions as I wrote this book. My dear friend Ashleigh Raper's first words when I mentioned my crazy idea to write this biography were 'I am so here for this book', and she was with me every step of the way. Also thank you to those people close to Berejiklian who spoke to me against her wishes. Despite Berejiklian being totally convinced that I was aiming to do a political hit job on her (of course, never my intention), many of her closest confidants saw the value in documenting the story of a hugely impressive woman who, like the rest of us, is flawed.

All authors thank their children, and with good reason. I was chained to my computer while my amazing kids went through some big changes; my eldest Xavier started high school and my baby Oscar went off to kindergarten. Meanwhile my husband, Justin, who completely accepts my love of politics, supported me every step of the way. And then there was my sassy middle child Annabel, who is wise beyond her years. At just nine, she was the one who kept telling me to stay focused and remember how proud I would feel when this book hits the shelves. Every day she told me to believe in myself. I look at Annabel and feel totally confident that there is a new generation of women, inspired by the likes of Grace Tame, who are storming their way through life, ready to take over the world. And I can't wait to see what they achieve.